THE RED CUP
Diaries

CD CASA

Dedication

This book is dedicated to my amazing children, my loving family, my beautiful grandkids, and to every reader who finds a piece of themselves within these chapters.

In loving memory of my dad.

Opening

There are times when I doubt that my story could help anyone, but this book has been in my heart and mind since the early 2000s. I've known the title of it since 2003. I've never uttered the title of it for fear I would see it advertised as a best seller, written by someone else. But this story is my truth and lived experience.

You can ask anybody addicted to any type of substance and/or dysfunctional lifestyle and they'll probably agree, it was never about a lack of love for our children.

To my precious children, it was never about not loving you. In fact, it was quite the opposite. Although I never planned to get pregnant with any of you, I've been pregnant three times, and I have you three to show for it. Each time I learned that I was pregnant, I made a conscious decision to have you and embrace motherhood. I know for many years, I failed miserably at making you feel safe and loved, but today I know I've shown you that my heart was always in it. There's nothing I wouldn't do for you three and, if I died today, I would be at peace, knowing that I've shown you, at the very least, that hard work and determination can change your whole life. My faith in God is my biggest anchor, and I hope the day will come when you too, will see His many miracles in our lives. It was never about the drugs and alcohol. My sack of baggage was so large and heavy. Filled with things from years before you came into my life and added to, in abundance, as the years rolled on. This bag was filled with hurt, abandonment, fear, rejection, insecurity, doubt, and intolerance of others. Today I can say that this bag is not only free of all these elements, but the bag I bring to the table today is filled with love, truth, confidence, patience, grace, mercy, hope, joy, and self-control.

I've asked my three children to write a few examples of the memories they have from my drinking days, basically their whole early childhood. Those memories, from their viewpoint, will be woven into this story. My story is told from the viewpoint of an alcoholic single mother battling a disease that was trying to take my life.

My biggest hope in writing this book is that anybody struggling with any kind of baggage, will be able to open this book, to any chapter, and know that there is light at the end of the tunnel. It's never too late to turn our life around. Most importantly, when we step out of self and into God's glorious plan for our life, we can experience more than we ever thought possible.

CHAPTER *1*

Just a Young Girl

*I*t was never really about the drugs and alcohol; it was the years of baggage that I'd been dragging with me since childhood. Thinking back, the first use would be hard to pinpoint, but I can sure remember some of the earliest times when baggage became part of my gear.

I remember the year my dad sat us down, each on one knee, and explained to us that he would be leaving. This took place less than a month after my brother was born in late November 1979, only a few days after Christmas. I can't imagine the dynamic that would've been flowing through our home and family as those weeks rolled on. But today I can recognize the little girl inside of me who knew that things were going to be changing.

Abandonment became one of my biggest anchors to the world I was always trying to escape. People leaving, people disappointing, not feeling safe, so unsure of what was going on in life, yet not being old enough or having the emotional intelligence to identify feelings or reality. You'd think that after experiencing this with the first man I loved, this would've been enough to spare myself from letting this happen again. It wasn't. I chose to fall in love with and have children with another man just like him.

I remember as a young woman, sitting on the kitchen floor of our home, crying, with a huge knot on my wrist. Jack had thrown me up against the wall that morning. It was always because I wanted to talk and get a few things straight. His answer was always to leave. That particular day, he'd decided to pick me up and forcefully move me out of his way. As I sat sobbing, looking at my hand and wrist, I realized I had to come up with a good story to excuse myself from court reporting school that day. I knew that no one would believe that I fell or tripped; the knot on my hand couldn't have happened that way.

There were many times during my early career when I had to make up excuses for my appearance due to being abused. There were far more times that I had to make up excuses for my behavior due to trying to hide all the chaos happening at home.

I learned this behavior very early on. My mother, a saint to all on the outside, taught us very early that if you appear to be okay, then in fact, things just really might be okay. Life as a child of an alcoholic and an enabler wound us in a web of lies, deceit, and fakeness. Of course, as a child, you want to, and tend to, believe things because it's your parents speaking it to you. Your parents speak it, the extended family accepts it, and we all get in the car and drive to the next episode of utter chaos.

I can say that pulling myself out of the chaos into reality was one of the scariest parts of obtaining the freedom I have today.

The pivotal point from chaos to calm can seem evident to others. But, in reality, it's an internal storm that eventually grows into a lifelong strength.

CHAPTER 2

My Hope

Throughout my years of bondage, drinking, using substances, putting up with nonsense, bitterness, and rage, I always knew that God was calling me to something more. There were many times that I didn't think I was worthy of living a different life. After all, I had put up with so much and put myself in these insane situations.

My hope and my reason for anyone reading this book is that you can open it to any chapter or page and find the hope you need to hang on for one more day. I want you to understand, that eventually, if you're one of the lucky ones, all these things you're going through will make sense one day. Today I can look back and know that it all had to happen that way for me to be who I am and where I am today. One step different to the left or to the right would've thrown me off track.

Back in my darkest days, I would get the kids to sleep and spend many hours, right on through to the early morning, listening to music and coming up with a plan to get us out of this mess. This went on for years, the music inspiring me, my faith in God so strong, and me being in complete bondage to the bottle. Each morning I would make a pot of coffee, mostly for the smell, shower, and drive to the liquor store. Yes, I went to the liquor store that opened at six a.m. daily. Then, throughout the day, depending on what was happening, I'd frequent my other local stores. There was one time in 2007 when the old man at my third favorite liquor store told me he wouldn't sell to me. How appalling! For the most part, all the other liquor stores in the area gave me credit that equaled 90% of my monthly income. Completely insane. How cute that my mother and sister even tried to tell my number-one liquor store owner not to sell to me. They had no clue. By that time, he and another store owner had become my personal friends and would come to my house on their off time.

People loved hanging out with me even in my darkest times. I can only think that it was the Light inside of me that they were attracted to. In fact, I'll never forget the first day I met Andrew, the owner of the liquor store closest to me. I walked in with the boys in a double stroller, and he said, "Wow, you are so happy." My reply was "Yes, it's the Jesus inside of me." This was in 1998, the first year of my nine-year love affair with the vodka bottle.

Of course, as time went on, many people occasionally would ask, "Are you okay? You don't look so good." I'd go on and on about the stress of being a single mother and, of course, the bitterness and rage regarding Jack was always prevalent in my life. But honestly, it was the vodka doing its business on my body.

Anyway, my hope is that if you are going through dark times, angry with your loved ones, putting up with things you'd never imagined dealing with, being so scared to make a change as it all seems too far out of reach, understand this: you too can pull through this. These days there are so many, and I mean, *so many* resources available, that you can't and don't have to do this alone.

It's funny because my first question to those dealing with any kind of addiction or hurt is "Do you want to get help?" This question must be asked because so many times our families want us to get help, and our loved ones think that by withholding money, children, housing, and resources from us, of course, we'll get better. This just isn't the case. Unless you are completely over the lifestyle and nonsense you are living in and through, then nothing anyone takes from you will matter. You have to completely come to the end of yourself and want that change. It's progress, not perfection, but your willingness to suit up and show up will make all the difference in the world.

CHAPTER 3

Meeting Jack

February 15, 1987, the day after Valentine's Day. There were so many signs. That Valentine's Day, both my bestie and I were single. We were invited to go over to Kaylee's house to party and hang out. It was rainy and cold, and we bundled up in our jeans, flannels, and high-top L.A. Gears. I bought myself a Valentine's balloon at the store and we picked up a couple of party favors. Kaylee had a crazy boyfriend who was experimenting with steroids. As the night went on, we were alerted to her boyfriend hiding out in the bushes. I remember telling my bestie, "I'm not sleeping with this going on." So, up all night, which was one of the many, we stayed inside and monitored the stalking of Kaylee's boyfriend.

The next morning it was still raining. My sister had left my mom's house a few weeks prior and was off with her new boyfriend. As my bestie and I set out for the day, with no shower and just the clothes we'd been in all night, we were set on finding my sister. I had a feeling I knew where to find her, and off we went. When we got to this one-star motel, there was the car I knew my sister had driven. We went to the door and indeed found my sister. She and her new boyfriend were just getting up and stepped into the other room to get dressed. As I and my bestie sat sifting through the morning newspaper, there was a knock on the door. I answered the door, and it was like a lightning bolt hit me. There he stood—Jack. The man I would live with, deal with, and have children with for the next decade. Of course, I didn't know all the heartache this would entail, but the mystery and the allure sucked me in like a vacuum.

Jack had, at the time, a woman who was pregnant and whom he claimed he didn't love, but he was there for her during her pregnancy. I remember hanging out with him, and him asking to kiss me. One of my biggest things was not messing with other women's men. So, I didn't. Within a few short weeks, this lady had her baby, which turned out to be twins. She'd had no prenatal care and had been using drugs the whole time. The babies were born three months early and I felt like it was a sign. Unfortunately, one of the babies didn't survive, and that whole trauma started, but at the time it wasn't my business or my trauma. Oh, what a fool. Jack and I began seeing each other and I felt like it was meant to be. My mom would always say, "I don't want you seeing this guy." What did she know? I mean, what was the problem? I was a senior in high school, and he was twenty-five years old. He was my first boyfriend who had a car, was adventurous, and strong, and as a bonus, he didn't drink. I never wanted to be with someone who was an alcoholic. I really should've set my standards higher than not drinking; it should've been: someone who doesn't use substances, who is emotionally available, and who would prove himself solid in the face of a crisis. But I didn't have the self-esteem to feel like I deserved any of that. Also, my emotional intelligence was on hold, as I was using by then, too. This would all be a subconscious error, but an error, nonetheless.

CHAPTER 4

More About Jack

While writing this book, I've allowed the Lord to guide me through each keystroke. I've been amazed at how the majority of the story has come out without throwing anybody under the bus. That is not the point of writing this book. The people in my life along the way have their own baggage, and I'm sure their own story, but none of that is my concern.

37,000 words into this, I realized that I should be more descriptive regarding my relationship with Jack for anyone who may think this road was easy.

When I met Jack, I was young and had the whole world at my fingertips. I had a great job and was full of life. I was also an insecure, damaged little girl who was looking for someone to love me. I trusted Jack. I shouldn't have, but I did. I wanted to trust him. I didn't know back then that people don't and won't love you the same just because you've given so much of yourself to them.

Not only was there another woman pregnant with his child, or children as it turned out to be but there were many other signs that told me to run. I was in my senior year of high school and a few months into knowing him, he came to live with me at my mom's house. Two red flags—the other woman, and the fact that he didn't have his own residence. But I continued to convince myself that he was a good guy.

The day I graduated from high school, Jack and my sister showed up as we were leaving. Neither of them had made it a point to be there for the ceremony. Two months after graduating from high school, Jack and I would move into our own little place.

I was the only one who was legitimately bringing in a paycheck, but he always had money. Back in those days, he had a brother who was wheeling and dealing on the side of his own business. Red flag number three; we were both using meth and marijuana. I'd still go to work each day like a 'normal' person. I loved working. It brought me great joy and I was very good at it.

Nobody at work knew that I had a boyfriend at home who didn't work, and nobody suspected any drug use. Jack didn't technically deal drugs, but he always had it and had a friend or two that would score from him.

Four months into living together, we shared our first Christmas. We had gone and picked out a tree, we bought an "Our first Christmas" ornament, and I was excited to have one big present under the tree already from him. We also had a triple-beam scale to weigh meth, in our hall closet on the shelf under the towels.

Now, although I was using, I hated that lifestyle. December 19, 1987, was a Saturday and I woke up with this feeling of dread. He was in the kitchen with one of his friends, and his brother came over. His brother had asked me what was wrong, and I told him my intention of giving Jack an ultimatum. When the company left I did just that. I pointed to the drug paraphernalia and told Jack, "Either that goes, or I go." He assured me that he only had a small bag left and that one of his friends would be picking it up later that day.

It was early evening and we had planned to do some Christmas shopping. We were waiting for his friend to come pick up the bag of meth and we'd be ready to go. His friend got there, and they sat in the kitchen for a few short minutes. The dope and the money were out on the table, and I heard footsteps—loud, pounding footsteps. Our little apartment had a sliding glass door as the front door, so I pulled back the curtain to take a peek.

There they were, several cops, sliding the door open, guns drawn. I screamed and jumped over Jack's leg to run to the corner of the kitchen. There was only one door in, and one door out, and we weren't going anywhere. They ordered us to sit on the couch while they proceeded to dump every drawer and ransack every closet looking for more dope.

They had all the evidence they needed sitting on the table. I cried and cried, and Jack apologized over and over. His friend knew what a neat freak I was and looked horribly sorry, too. That night, I'd spend two hours in the little city jail, waiting to be released. There were only a few cells in this jail, and I sat on the very edge of the bar of the bed just terrified at this turn of events. About half an hour before they drove me back home, I realized Jack was in the cell next to me. He went on and on about how sorry he was and promised it would never happen again.

I went home and called my bestie, and we spent the next several hours trying to put my home back together. Jack was released the next day and we went on with our lives. The court case would go on for the next two years. I ended up doing six months of probation while Jack was sentenced to some little camp up in the mountains for six weeks.

I did get to see what that Christmas present was, early. The cops had ripped the wrapping off of it. It was a fancy typewriter, the new kind with the built-in whiteout.

At the time, I worked for this same city. I was still doing temporary work in multiple departments, and I'd hoped and prayed that people wouldn't know what had happened in my life over the weekend. I was very naïve. Nobody ever said anything, but they didn't have to. The shame and guilt I was carrying were enough to ruin anything that may have been good.

By the middle of the following year, I had been hired in a permanent position for the city. I was still able to keep up the façade of living a normal life. Now Jack's brother was my sister's boyfriend. He had his own business and was a very successful businessman. They were also in the fast life.

Every night after work, I'd come home to an empty house as Jack was always with my sister. This went on for years but knowing that I came from a bloodline of jealous people, I did my best to let things fly. It drove me crazy. The hurt and abandonment were refueled daily by their behavior and actions.

Why didn't my sister want to be with me and why wasn't he home with me?

My sister and her boyfriend had gotten into a fight, and she decided to rent a hotel room. She called me and asked me to bring her food. I don't remember why my car wasn't working but I had called a friend and asked her to drive me. We were just going to drop off food as my friend couldn't be out long. This particular friend didn't use drugs either, so a ride was all she was available for.

When we got to the hotel room, my sister was just getting out of the shower. I asked her if she wanted to come to my house for the night and she said no and that she'd be fine. As we turned to leave there was a knock on the door. It was Jack. He had come to "check on her" and said he'd be home later.

Again, trying to restrain my bloodline of jealousy, I left with my friend, and she dropped me off at home. Around two a.m., Jack's brother called. I ranted and raved about the whole incident, and he said, "I'm coming to get you." We drove by the hotel and sure enough, there were my sister and Jack's cars, still tucked in the underground parking lot. I urged Jack's brother to park so we could go confront them and he said, "Nah, let's get some food." I wanted to jump out of the truck and go give them a piece of my mind, but I stayed in the car.

We grabbed some food and headed home. Jack's brother dropped me off and I sat alone, in the middle of the night, knowing I had a big decision to make.

Somewhere I had found a huge box. My mom still lived over on the next block and my plan was to drag this box, with most of my belongings, up around the corner and go back to live with my mom. Oh, how I should've gone; that decision would've changed my whole life.

I had spent the morning putting my clothes and things in this box and Jack arrived home around eleven a.m. I had been crying all night and I was exhausted. He walked in surprised that I was packing. I informed him that I was leaving and going back home. Here it came again, "Baby, baby, please don't leave. I'm so sorry. Please stay and we'll work this out."

Oh, what a fool. This was definitely a fork in the road, and I should've followed my original plan. But I didn't. I remember going to his family gatherings and watching his brothers and their wives. I continuously told myself to get out of this relationship before I got pregnant, but time has a funny way of getting away from you when you're in denial.

I got pregnant the following month. When I was in high school and all the other kids were talking about where they'd go to college and what they planned on being when they grew up, I would ask myself what it was I wanted to do. My job with the city was already laid out for me and this was a huge blessing. But, in my heart, I wanted to be a court reporter. I was born to be a court reporter.

Sitting on my lunch break one day at work, I took out a piece of paper and started to figure out the financial aspect of having a child. I allotted for rent, diapers, food, and all of the necessities of having a child. These figures, of course, had to fit in with only my income, as Jack never had a steady job. When I completed my estimated expenses, I saw that I would still have a couple hundred dollars to spare each month, and I made the decision that day to have this baby.

It hadn't been part of my plan, but I knew that I needed to take responsibility for my actions, and I threw myself into becoming a mom. I would continue to work up into my ninth month of pregnancy. I was young, healthy, and had a great job so insurance and such were covered.

I had my first child, a baby girl, three days after my twentieth birthday. I was in love. I would've done anything for this little girl, and I quickly learned how to be a mom and protector. Jack still wasn't working but he also was never home. He'd come and go as he pleased, and I would just deal with it.

When my maternity leave was up, I made plans with both my mom and Jack's mom as I worked on the weekends. Each morning I'd get up, take my baby to his mother's house, go to work, and pick my baby up at the end of each day. I remember asking him if he'd be willing to help with the drop-offs, but nothing was ever stable with him.

I breastfed for a couple of months and once I stopped, I started using again. Alcohol wasn't an issue back then, we didn't drink. But a little bit of meth and marijuana were a daily thing. I continued to work for the next year and a half, and I just felt so sad. I was torn between two loves, my job and my daughter. The people I worked with were bitter and malicious and I'd come home in tears sometimes over the office politics.

Jack kept telling me to quit. He'd say, "I'll take care of you guys," and for some insane reason, I believed him. After requesting a department transfer, the only two options were the library and the police department. I couldn't picture myself in a quiet library and I couldn't possibly put myself in the police department; they knew who we were.

One day I made the decision to resign and decided I'd go to court reporting school. Signing that piece of paper was sealing my fate, but I didn't know any better, nor did I have any type of guidance from my parents.

I began court reporting school and for the most part, we'd established that Jack would be the stay-at-home dad. This of course was hit and miss because he wasn't dependable. I missed many days of school but was enjoying every minute of my new career. I was learning so much and enjoying the typing part of it. My brain and my body felt in sync with my destiny.

Over the next year, I was trying to establish another career with school and future jobs in this field. I'd be done with school within another year and a half, and I was excited for what the future held.

Having Jack as the daycare provider proved to be a complete nightmare. Not only would I come home to him and all his friends playing Nintendo, but there'd be several signs that unwelcome guests had been there. Jack would tell me I was crazy and that everything was fine. I knew better. As long as my child was taken care of, I sucked it up and continued to attempt to build a future for us.

Some of my girlfriends, whom I'd known for years, were also coming to the house when I wasn't home. They were coming for the meth, and I knew it. I'd ask Jack about this, and he'd tell me I was imagining things. Questioning Jack would always turn into a fight, and I always ended up sounding and feeling like I was losing my mind.

I'd also gotten to the point where I'd ask my friends if they'd been over, and they'd lie straight to my face. One day I came home to the sheets and the comforter in the dryer. Jack never did housework, so I knew something was up. Jack was sleeping with my friends while I was at school, and I decided that I wasn't going to put up with this. *I'll quit school and guard the house* was my thinking.

So, I did. I put school on hold and decided to be a stay-at-home mom. This proved to be another decision that would seal my fate into a world of nothing. We had nothing, no steady income, no stable relationship, and certainly no positive parenting skills. The only thing I had was my love for my daughter and my faith in God.

Within a few short months, I decided to move out. I took my daughter and got another place, thinking, "Certainly, he'll get a job and fight for us. He doesn't want to lose his girls." Wrong again. He didn't do a damned thing about it. He turned our cute little duplex into a Nintendo bachelor pad and continued on with his life.

At this point, I was now on public assistance and the shame that came with that was weighing on me more than I knew. I tried to move on with my life, but Jack would still come around. He wasn't there for anything stable, but I couldn't seem to resist him when he popped in and out of our lives. I was stuck in this web of lies and manipulation.

My daughter and I ended up moving back home several months later only to jump right back into the chaos and periodic domestic violence. We finally lost that little duplex due to a lack of funds. I stayed with a friend for a bit and even went back home to my mother for a while. One of her stipulations was that I didn't see Jack anymore, but that seemed impossible at the time.

For so many years, Jack was never home. Throughout these years, I had many friends who encouraged and valued me, so I leaned toward these friends. One night after being at my friend's house, enjoying music and some fun, I went home in the middle of the night. I put my daughter in bed and was sitting in the living room reading the newspaper. At the time, we lived in that cute little duplex with an enclosed patio attached. As I sat reading, I thought I heard something move around out on the patio. This was only the beginning of the years I would be losing sleep trying to protect my children. About an hour had passed, and I kept my ears peeled, knowing I wasn't imagining things and then an alarm on a watch went off outside. My motherly instinct was to grab a weapon and confront this intruder head-on. I grabbed a hammer, turned on the patio light and there he was. Jack, the man who was supposed to be protecting us, sitting in the corner of our patio. He instantly got up and started to yell at me to put the hammer down. I was furious. I shouted, "Why didn't you just come in? Why are you trying to scare me?" His only reply was, "I just thought I'd tell you how well Kim's legs wrapped around me, how great she was to me." *Really, is that what your intention of lurking was?* I was beside myself, as I would be many more times in the coming years.

Again, all those feelings of abandonment and mistrust came rushing back. *Why am I doing this to myself? I've got to let him go.*

Only a crazy person would allow this to continue, but I knew in my heart that I was alone in this. No restraining order would ever be enough with Jack. He was too sneaky and knew exactly how to instill fear in me and keep me in bondage.

CHAPTER 5

The Nightmare Continues

I ended up getting a house with a friend I'd known since elementary school. He loved my daughter, and we were great friends. I was still on public assistance, and he worked full-time. We started to develop feelings for each other, but I could never pull myself away from the allure of Jack.

One day my friend came home from work and Jack was there. My friend was pissed. He couldn't understand why I'd allowed him to come over, but I was set on giving Jack all the chances he needed to be a father and a partner. It was all a complete fantasy as this was never going to be the case.

Jack and I ended up moving into an apartment where he knew the manager. This place was in a bad neighborhood, and it seemed as if everyone there was on public assistance and content to be. I don't know why I ever put the safety and security of my daughter and myself back in Jack's hands, but I wanted to believe things could be different.

We continued to fight all the time as he was never home. He'd be out with this person or that chick or doing whatever he wanted to do. Of course, he'd label me jealous or crazy or tell me I was asking too much of him. I finally decided it was time to make a bold move and that night I tried on some clothes to make sure I had a wardrobe suitable for a job. I planned to back to work and get us out of this. That night I ended up getting pregnant again.

I was devastated and disappointed in myself. How could I have let this happen again? But, as was my nature, I decided to accept things and make the best of it. My daughter was old enough to know that there was another baby on the way, and she was not happy about it. She was living in a world of hell and even at her young age, I think she was scared for this new baby, too.

My first son would be born in December of 1995. During my pregnancy, Jack was never home. Nothing new, but this time I didn't have any plan at all. I just knew that I needed to focus on bringing a healthy baby into the world. I was terrified, as I knew I had nothing to offer this child. The week we brought our son home, Jack left us at home. We had three tortillas, two potatoes, and an almost empty carton of milk. He was gone for three weeks.

I know this sounds crazy, but it was normal. He'd always say, "I'll be right back," and literally days and weeks would go by before he'd return. Thank God for my mother who would bring us a few things, but she was beyond worried about us. She was angry with me for getting myself in this situation and she was protective over my children and the conditions we were living in.

I was a mess. Two children had died in this complex around the time my son was born. One of them was murdered by the child's family and the other died of sudden infant death syndrome (SIDS). This freaked me out more than life itself. I was not sleeping well at all. I kept the kids close to me and checked their breathing throughout the night. The internal fight in me was hitting an all-time high and I was just about to push the envelope of life.

Those next several months were excruciating. When Jack would come home he'd fall asleep within thirty minutes and when he'd wake up, he'd shower and leave again. I wanted answers. I wanted to know where he was going and who he was with.

There was this guy named Franco who would come by to check on me periodically. He had grown up in this neighborhood and knew everybody. Jack had another brother who lived in the neighborhood too, and one night I asked our niece to watch the kids. Franco helped me take all the laundry to the laundromat, which gave us a few hours to chat. This was when he informed me that Jack was hanging out, most of the time, in one of the apartments in the complex. I had no idea he was only a few doors over and still couldn't come to check on us.

When we got back home, Franco and I had sex. I guess I was so grateful that I now had some answers and Franco was just sweet and kind to me. I made him use a condom as I wasn't trying to get pregnant again.

By August of that year, my body was feeling different. I knew the feeling. My breasts were aching, and I was in denial about the reason behind it. I knew I was pregnant again. I went to the clinic to get confirmation and sure enough, another baby was on the way. I was terrified. How could I have let this happen again? I decided that I could not have another baby. I knew what my family would say as I couldn't even feed the ones I had.

For fear that this was Franco's baby, I sat Jack down one day and explained what had happened. I assured him that I'd made an appointment to get an abortion. One of my neighbors took me to the appointment and my spirit was just crushed. I prayed for the Lord to forgive me, and I knew that I'd have a lifelong weight on my shoulders.

I put the flimsy little patient's robe on, and the nurse did an ultrasound to check how far along I was. When she informed me that I was a couple of months along, I quickly realized that this couldn't have been Franco's baby. I hadn't even known him that long. I sat up and exclaimed that I didn't want to go through with this procedure.

I came rushing through the door at home, grabbed my calendar, and was so excited. Jack was watching the kids that day and he was curious about why I was so excited. I explained to him how far along I was, showed him on the calendar the time frame that conception would've happened, and was thrilled to tell him that this was our baby. I was going to have the baby. I was so relieved that I didn't have to abort this child.

I was so ecstatic, and I suggested he take the kids to the park while I prepared tacos for us. Jack was not as happy as I was. He didn't care what happened to us, but he certainly didn't like the fact that I'd been so honest about my infidelity. As far as he was concerned, this baby wasn't his. I knew it was and that was all that mattered to me.

Next came telling my family and my daughter. I'll never forget the way my daughter sat in my lap and cried that night. She was so angry. Even at seven years old, she kept saying, "You just had a baby; this is the worst thing ever." It really was but I knew, in my heart of hearts, that somehow, we'd get through this. And I knew, that not aborting a child was better for my soul and mind in the long run.

My mom was also angry. She was doing everything she could to provide diapers and food and it was so hard for her to watch how these children were being raised.

Our daily life was a mess. I'd walk my daughter to school and come home to half-ass tend to my infant. I knew that I'd taken the very limits of life and pushed it to the edge. I also knew that I would have some very hard decisions to make in the very near future.

I took on this fight-or-flight mentality and became internally strong to get through this. I knew deep in my spirit that life was about to take a drastic turn. Jack was never around, and I was exhausted all the time. I knew there was only one way out and that was to make it through. Against my strongest desire and beliefs, I used meth three or four times while I was pregnant. I was so sad and overwhelmed. There will never be a good excuse for it, but I needed to have energy for my other two children.

One of the times I used was two days before giving birth, in April 1997. Back at the same hospital that I'd just delivered at in December of '95, I knew I was in a world of shit. I had the same doctor who'd delivered my other son, and I was comfortable with him. As I was giving birth I informed him of the meth use, and he assured me that we'd take care of it once the baby was out. My third child was born healthy and beautiful. He was also born with traces of drugs in his system, otherwise known as 'positive tox.'

I had really screwed up this time and everybody knew it. There would be no hiding this one. My family knew, Jack's family knew, and the authorities knew. I had dug a hole so deep, and I knew only God could get us out of this. I obviously wasn't reliable or capable. God's grace was with us the whole time, though it took me years to see it.

CHAPTER 6

Treatment

How many times have I done treatment? I'll try to report an accurate count. My first treatment would've been when I was pregnant with my third child. This was an outpatient program for women. I remember lugging the baby seat with me and dragging my precious little seven-year-old too when she wasn't in school. Things like carrying, by hand, a car seat with an infant in it, can really turn you off from wanting to zip out the door and get to treatment. Or we tell ourselves that. It's actually the cunning disease of addiction that'll tell you, "Oh! You broke a shoelace? You should try again tomorrow." Or "Wow! I'm in the middle of doing the laundry, if I get this done, life will be better." It's all a delusion to avoid facing the root cause of the addiction and dysfunction. Obviously, this would be the first of many treatment attempts.

Next would come when my third child was born positive tox. I'd only used meth three or four times throughout this pregnancy, but I did use. I admitted it to the doctor as he was delivering my baby. There's no excuse for it and this will always be one of my most private memories I've chosen to share. If you want to judge me, go ahead. Nothing I do today is for your approval or sympathy. I had just had a baby, my second child, and had a child in early elementary school. Jack was out stealing top-of-the-line bicycles by this point and hanging out with other chicks who approved of his actions. It was terrifying in this particular apartment complex we lived in, surrounded by drugs and the knowledge of the death of those two babies, well aware of what fresh hell awaited me regarding getting us out of this mess.

When kiddo number three was born, mid-afternoon, they let me bottle-feed him at the hospital throughout the night. The next morning, they came into my room and informed me that I could leave, but not with him. My mom came to get me and was furious. As we walked out of the hospital, there was my precious baby, in the bassinet smack dab in the middle of the nurse's station. They waved goodbye and gave me the phone number of a social worker to contact. My mom barked at me to get in the car. My other two children were at my mom's house. She dropped me off at home and said, "Figure it out." I walked to the liquor store and bought wine coolers. Alcohol wasn't the substance I often used, at this point, but I needed something to help me figure it out. I showered and sat on my living room floor. I started to pull out the sheets of referrals I had been given from the past treatment program, or elsewhere. I had a whole list of programs for women, but very few of them had anything to offer where you could bring your children with you.

It is here that I'll say thank you to my mother and Jack's sister who took care of my baby those first few months of his life. My mom had just retired from her former place of employment: she had a new job now. My newborn did go to a foster home for the first five days of his life. I've never met that person, nor do I know how to backtrack and find them. But for all of this help, I'm so grateful. Again, God always had his hand on us, and the miracles are too numerous to count.

For the next couple of months, I tried to attend self-help meetings and remain sober. The social worker who would call and come to the house was a very scary woman. She was not soft or gentle in any sense of the word. Daily I would call these programs to find out where we could go. I was not going to do outpatient treatment. That wouldn't have worked. I wanted to go somewhere that I could take my children and have my third join us. He was born in April 1997 and it wasn't until August 1997 that we would pack up the house, put everything we owned in storage, and check ourselves into residential treatment.

The relationship my mother and I had was so off balance for so many years. Her concern was soft, cozy bedding for us to take into the treatment center. My concern was leaving a life of utter chaos. My third baby was able to join us in residential treatment two months after entering and things went as smoothly as possible for the next year. This was a faith-based treatment facility where they taught us about God and the possibilities for those who believe. I had always been a believer. I had known as a young child that there was something bigger than life itself Who was guiding me and watching every move I made. It was always so powerful that I shied away from It. But I knew. I remember them telling us that anything you asked for from the Lord could come true if you believed it in your heart. This particular program had what they called 'graduate housing.' I would look up at the second story of this building, knowing that carrying a baby on each hip, up those stairs, was going to be insanely hard.

Toward my tenth month in the program, I went to a program off-site to arrange for the next step in my journey. This other program offered two things: housing and job search help. My intention was to find a job so we could move out and on with our lives. While I was waiting for someone from the residential program to pick me up, there was a gentleman named Tony who was walking through the parking lot. I had no idea that Tony was actually in charge of their housing component. We exchanged pleasant hellos and went our separate ways. When I returned to the facility where we lived, the program manager called me into her office. She informed me that Tony had called. Their program was given one Section 8 voucher per year and he wanted me to have it! Miracles, as you'll read, happened all throughout my years of living. So, for those who wonder where I found this rock-solid faith, it's from walking through and living this hard yet so rewarding life.

The other women in the program were shocked. They couldn't grasp what had happened and how I had gotten this blessing. My only comeback was, "They taught us that anything is possible and that if you ask for it, it will be given to you." They weren't buying it, but I didn't care. A full-blown blessing had fallen into my lap and I was going to enjoy every minute of it.

My biggest goal for writing this book is to lay it all out there. Every flaw, every fear, every mistake, every truth so that anyone struggling will know, you're not the only one. There will come a time when it will all make sense. Every relapse, every bad day, every trauma-filled experience that we go through, is a puzzle piece of your journey.

While in this residential program, once we'd been there a while, we mothers would take turns walking the school-aged children to the elementary school a few blocks away. There wasn't much in this shady part of town other than some industrial businesses and run-down houses and, smack-dab at the halfway mark was... you guessed it, a liquor store. Sometimes we'd stop with the kids and let them buy snacks and candy, so it wasn't like we weren't allowed in the store. Twice, while at my residential stay, I bought a tiny bottle of vodka and took it back to my room. I had no clue that the lurking bottle of vodka would become my biggest downfall in the coming years. Either way, I felt so guilty about taking a shot or two and would dwell for days on how to get this bottle out of my room.

After doing a full year of residential treatment, my children and I moved out into a beautiful three-bedroom, two-bath home. It had a front and back yard, and a garage for storage and laundry. It had an additional room that became the kid's playroom. The elementary school was only a few blocks away. Yes, this elementary school would be the same one that'll be referred to in so many other parts of this story, including the night the chains were broken.

The week leading up to going into residential treatment was a complete nightmare. When I mentioned putting all my belongings in storage, it was much more than that. Moving can be a total hardship under normal circumstances. There was nothing normal about these circumstances or the people around me. We lived upstairs and Jack was nowhere to be found to help. A family member had a small Ford truck with a camper shell on it so the loads I was taking to storage were limited by space. Up and down the stairs I went, all week, by myself. The night before the big day came, I had my two children who were asleep in the bedroom. I must've been so exhausted that I fell asleep in the living room. Around ten p.m. I woke up and realized that I hadn't showered before falling asleep. Again, the whole week of moving had taken a toll. I only had the bedroom furniture (which I was giving to my neighbor) and the items we were taking with us into treatment. When I woke up, I wanted to rinse off before going back to sleep. I started the bath water and went back to the living room. The sound of water has always been one of my most relaxing sounds and comforts. You guessed it. I fell back asleep. Approximately an hour and a half later I was startled awake to someone pounding on my door. It was my neighbor underneath me. She was screaming and yelling about water coming in through her ceiling. I was disoriented and confused. And then I heard the water running. Oh, how my heart sank. She continued to yell and said she was calling the cops. I walked down the short hallway to the bathroom, squish, squish, squish, and turned the water off. I couldn't believe it, another major mistake before stepping into a solution. With the front door open, I sat on a large box and just sobbed. All the anger and bitterness of Jack not being there to help came rushing in. That, and I never wanted to burden others. The firemen showed up to assess the place, went to check the bedroom where the kids were sleeping, and found that we'd be stable until the next day. Of course, the neighbors had to leave. I recall the neighbor shouting about the new furniture she had just purchased. We only knew each other by face but I still felt terrible. The next morning after handing my weed pipe to my neighbor, the last thing I did before leaving that awful complex was leave a note on the neighbor's door that read, "I'm very sorry that my dysfunctional life has had an impact on you and your family."

28

CHAPTER 7

A New Start

The first few months in our beautiful new home took some getting used to. I had never been in a home this big with my children and had never had a yard or laundry right at my fingertips. Little by little, I started to feel that I should relish in the blessing. I would push the boys in a very heavy two-seater stroller to walk my daughter to school and things seemed to be getting more comfortable. Within a couple of months, my landlord had a small Geo Metro for sale. It was a great little car, and the price was right. When I say little, I mean little, with an eleven-year-old in the front seat and two car seats in the back. But it got us around and it was better than trying to maneuver that heavy stroller. Blessings were flowing all around, but that tiger was just waiting for my baggage to tear open.

A few of the girls I was in the residential treatment program with had also moved out of treatment and one in particular was living fairly close to me. She had six kids and our children had become friends while in treatment. One day when taking my daughter over to spend the night, she asked me if I knew where to get any meth. She was using again. The details are fuzzy, but I ended up at some guy's house going to score for my friend. It was in a brief conversation with him that he mentioned his mechanic, and I realized this was an old friend of mine from elementary school. I was so excited to be able to reconnect with people from a simpler time in my life. I left my phone number for Brad to call me. Brad did call. He too was excited to get together and catch up. Brad used drugs and I knew this, but I had no intention to start using again. I just needed some normalcy in my life and felt safe with Brad around. Within a few weeks, Brad was staying the night frequently and we would party and 'hang out.' Basically, Brad was living with us but I didn't think of it like that until it was too late. It was also around this time that I needed to go to the dentist. The dentist has always been my kryptonite, terrifying and intruding, to say the least. Even as a young child, my mom tells a story about trying to take me to the dentist. Sprawled out, both arms and legs across the entry door, the dentist wasn't ever a place I could handle going to on my own.

A few doors away from our new home was a liquor store. The first time I went in there was in the morning after walking my daughter to school. I'll never forget what the owner said: "Wow, who are you? You have such a light and happiness about you." "It's the light of the Lord" was my reply. So here I had a dental appointment, and my intention was to take the edge off. I went into the store and bought a half-pint of vodka. After all, it's the only alcohol that people can't smell, right? Right. Until it's coming out of your pores. This wasn't supposed to be an ongoing habit, but, between Brad being around and me actually purchasing the alcohol, the baggage now had a tear in it. Not to mention, my spirit was guilty, and my disease was in cover-up mode.

That one half-pint turned into many more. I still had boxes in my bedroom closet as I hadn't put everything from storage away. That was where I would keep the bottle, tucked under whatever was in the box. "This isn't a problem, but it doesn't need to be in the kitchen cabinet," is what I'd tell myself. Besides, I was going to work through this, and no one, other than God, needed to know about it. Oh, the lies we tell ourselves. The justification and rationalization that we addicts can come up with.

Soon, everything seemed like it was falling into place. I had a job, had found adequate daycare, and my daughter was doing well in school. Brad was still around, and that toxic relationship was taking on a whole life of itself. I would use a little meth, go to work, and drink when I got home. Many people have a drink when they get home from work. But for me, it was more than that. There were days at work when I'd become bored or distracted and this is when the drinking started to become all

I'd think about. Not so much the drinking, but the drinking and how I could do both, work and drink. I was starting to believe that I could function in life and have a love affair with a monster. Anyone who is caught up in the dysfunction of addiction will tell you that it's time-consuming to dance with this monster. It consumes so much of you, but you don't realize it until after you can step away from it.

CHAPTER 8

Old Habits Creeping In

My job required me to go to the post office mid-day to retrieve orders from a post office box. This was a perfect opportunity to get out of the office for a nice little drive. I couldn't even believe myself the day I took a right instead of a left. I kept thinking, "All these little strip malls, there's got to be a liquor store here somewhere." And sure enough, I had found one. The guilt of pulling into the parking lot, the deep thought of what I would mix it with, all of this, planned within a five-minute timeframe. This would be one of the many pivotal points of where my life was headed.

My supervisor was a woman I had worked with a few years prior and she would always tell me, "I don't know how you do it. I couldn't leave my children to come to work every day." Nobody at work seemed to notice the smell of alcohol or the difference in me. My work performance was always right on point, so I guess maybe they didn't want to know or believe it. I certainly didn't want to believe I was pulling all these red flags into my life. After a couple of short months of this mail run becoming my mid-day drink, I felt like it was coming to a dangerous point. Driving home drinking, I would pick up the kids and act like it was a normal day. I know my babysitter was concerned. She was amazing. Great to my kids while gently trying to let me know that she could indeed see there was a problem.

One day, while sitting and staring at my kids' picture on my desk, I informed my supervisor that she was right. I couldn't be away from the kids anymore. I excused myself, thanked them for the opportunity, and went home to tend to the one relationship that was becoming most important, my love affair with the vodka bottle.

By now, my neighbor who lived next door and I had become friends and we had such different lives. She had a son who was my daughter's age, and they went to the same school. This was our initial bond but there would be more. She was married and seemed to have a normal life. But she used meth. Her husband who went to work every day had no idea that she used meth. This was a perfect cover-up for hanging out with her. Plus, I really liked her. She was fun and wise in so many ways. She was having an affair with her dope dealer and would go see him at night. But she'd be home in the morning to get her son ready for school and her husband off to work. This worked out perfectly for both of us. Each morning, after the kids left for school, she'd walk over with her little basket. It sounds funny but it truly was a little basket. A picnic full of chaos. In this basket was her meth pipe, and whatever other little trinkets she'd have gathered for that day. We'd sit in my room and talk about life, motherhood, and men, all the topics we both were failing at. Of course, I'd be drinking but it felt normal to have a buddy who was pretending things were okay in her world too.

It wasn't long before her husband was on to her. I mean, where was she actually going at night? One evening, they were screaming and yelling and ended up at the end of my driveway. The next thing we knew, she threw a rock at my kitchen window and broke one of the windowpanes. She was yelling something about me telling her husband about her affair. It wasn't me. After all, I had my own façade that I was so busy trying to cover up. This would be the end of our little mornings together. She got clean. I kept drinking.

In the next several weeks, Brad, who was living with me and my children for free, was starting to get fed up with my drinking. "You're drinking too much, you're a mess, you're hard to be around." It seemed as though it was always fine for others to use and/or drink, but not me. Today I can look back at this and know this was true. I was never meant to live that life. It had taken on a life of its own. I can also look back and see God's hand over every piece of my life and am so grateful for His mercy and His grace.

One day Brad decided he'd had enough, and he left. I remember sitting there, crying, wondering where we'd gone wrong, and hoping he'd come back. Talk about insanity. This wasn't ever meant to be a relationship and it was founded on dysfunction and addiction. I worked through it and decided I'd go back to school. All the while, my real relationship was in full bloom and being watered daily.

As the weeks rolled on, I felt like I was on a decent path. I mean, I was meeting the requirements the State had put on anyone receiving aid and the school was closer than my previous job, so I felt more comfortable with the kids being in daycare. Plus, I rarely stayed the whole day. I would use excuses like 'the kids have an appointment,' 'I don't feel that great,' etc. Whatever it took to nurture my love affair. I was taking a clerical class learning Word or Excel, hard to remember. This was at an inner-city location of a continuing education center. Back in those days, it was a mix of all the new cultures that were making their way into San Diego. I blended right in; no one would notice my dysfunction with all these other people around. One day, when getting into the elevator, a lady from another country, who could barely speak English asked me, "Have you been drinking?" She was embarrassed by her forthcoming remark and I, of course, as I often did, replied, "No, it must be left over from last night." This only lasted so long. One morning I had a few minutes to spare and decided to boil a few eggs before I left. I must've spent those few minutes trying to cover up my lies and drinking, and I flew out the door and left for school. When I came home for lunch and pulled up in the driveway I could hear what sounded like a fire alarm going off. Lo and behold, I had left the eggs boiling and they had been cooking for three hours. I went inside, turned off the alarms, and stood and looked at my mess. Eggs had exploded all over the ceiling, backsplash—everywhere. I was so grateful there hadn't actually been a fire; God's grace was all over my life! It was a great excuse to not go back for the afternoon session. I poured a drink and started to clean up my mess.

So many times, God did for me what I couldn't possibly do for myself, but I knew the time was coming that I'd have to face this demon that was taking over my life. We lived in that house for four years. Thankfully, all four houses we lived in during those ten years, I was never evicted. The first house, my landlord's son was getting out of the Army, and he was going to need his house back for them to live in. With the second condo, my landlord got a divorce and was selling the condo. With the third house, they too were getting a divorce, and the last house, well, we moved out due to extenuating circumstances, which will be explained in the next few treatment stories.

During the four years of living in this house, I tried to get sober on my own. I would half-ass attend self-help meetings and attempt to pull it together a few days. Obviously, it didn't take long for my mother to catch on to the drinking and it was always a race to hide it from her. It was another façade because she grew up with alcoholic parents and married a functional alcoholic. My disease didn't care. I did though, and it was always an internal battle.

I went to detox twice while living in that house. I'd reach out to my mom, tell her I needed to get help, and we'd come up with a plan for her to watch the kids while I went into detox. The first time was terrifying but only on the first day. It sounds crazy but I always loved being in detox. I felt like I was taking steps to address an obvious problem and it was like summer camp for adults. The first time, I did the four-day detox and what they called ten-day back then. It was an additional ten days of all-day classes to teach us about our addiction. We had class, chores, and meals with the same group of people. The worst part was the self-help meetings they held on-site. They'd put all of us from detox in one area and when the meeting started, they'd pull back this large curtain for all to see who was in detox.

I don't care what anybody says; when you're surrounded by people who are cut from the same cloth, you just feel at home. During our chores, we'd laugh and giggle about how messed up our lives were. I met some of the nicest people during these times.

The second trip to detox didn't work out so well. I planned on doing all fourteen days, but they'd send us on these long walks intended to be healthy for us. It was mid-summer, and I had some jean overalls on. One of the main ladies who ran the place confronted me and told me my shorts were too short. They were right above my knee, and I was totally not going to tolerate this. I couldn't help but stare at the four long hairs coming out of her chin. She also had a very nice ring on her wedding finger, and I couldn't fathom how someone could put a ring on her and not request that she pluck those hairs. All part of a distraction, just like breaking a shoelace. I refused to change my clothes, decided I didn't need to put up with this, and made my way back home.

CHAPTER 9

Trying to Gain Ground

My heart and my soul wanted to be sober. I wanted to be a good mother and a good woman. Today I know that there was both, locked inside a body that was working through years of baggage. Nothing lasted for long in the sobriety realm for me. It was always a few weeks without alcohol and then I'd smoke a joint or something else, and boom, the animal was alive again. The few friends I had would even comment that they liked me better when I wasn't drinking. I liked myself more too, but I still hadn't and wouldn't deal with the core issues. Back in those days, I continued to add to my baggage by not setting firm boundaries with Jack. He'd say he was going to pick up the kids for the weekend and never show. This happened often and it would infuriate me. There were times when he would hang up on me and I'd drive to his house to "set him straight." God's grace again. How I never ended up in jail or in an accident had to be something much larger than me watching over me.

I was always trying to be a good mom. For most of my drinking career, I would assume that if the house was clean, there was food on the table and the laundry was done, things would be okay. My mom would tell me that she could tell by the condition of my house if I was doing okay. I also prided myself on the fact that my house wasn't a party house. I had a select few friends who would come and hang out with me. But, for the most part, nothing happened in my children's home that I would have to hide from them. I didn't have men staying the night, I didn't have people coming to party in our living room, and I certainly didn't let people come and stay when they didn't have a place to go.

Another thing that always amazed me was that people would leave their children with me as if it were a safe place to be. One day I decided to take the boys fishing at the local lake. I had this lady's teen girl and her boyfriend with us. As we walked to find our fishing spot, I took a step on the scattered tree bark and my ankle snapped. I fell on my butt and couldn't walk on it. The boyfriend carried me to the car and was able to drive my little stick shift home. Fishing never happened. This was mid-afternoon and I had called the doctor to schedule a cast for the next day. The next morning the doorbell rang; I crawled to the door to answer it and it was my landlord delivering the news that his son was getting out of the Army and he would need the house back the following month. Looking back, I know the broken ankle was a blessing in disguise too. Had I had both legs working, I would've created an even bigger mess than what I was already in. I had my couple of friends in the neighborhood who would come help with housework during these weeks. They really should teach people how to use crutches in elementary school. I didn't have much choice but to sit and navigate a plan for our next move.

Within a couple of weeks, while hobbling around on crutches, I had found a place about two miles away. It was a three-story condo that had a pool in the complex. It was very nice and clean. I went to look at this place with a newly removed cast and the lady who owned it was open to taking the Section 8 voucher. Of course, I hadn't really thought it through with the stairs and the young children, but I was looking for safety and quality and this place had both.

It wasn't long before we got settled in and started to learn our new routine. Moving is always a major job and this wouldn't be any different. By this time, my daughter's bus stop for junior high was up around the corner and the boys were attending the elementary school. It was also around this time that my mom and stepdad decided to sell their home, buy an RV, and start traveling.

During their move, it became utter chaos. My stepdad and I were still not on great terms. He wasn't a very nice man until many years later, but he would do whatever my mom asked of him. As their move progressed, my mom would call and say he was on his way with a few things for us. He would pull up, attitude full-blast, and start tossing crap in my garage. I would call my mom and say, "Why are you sending all this stuff over?" Sending crap home, or over, was always a trigger for me. Either way, I couldn't stop it. It was what my mother wanted, and my resentment grew.

This would be the second time my mother had abandoned me. My mom had remarried during my ninth-grade year. This guy was getting some degree in computers back in those days. The computer thing never panned out and he ended up enlisting in the military. So, as my most crucial years of high school were approaching, my mom told us they were getting transferred to Germany. "How exciting! We finally get to see some of the world. It'll be great!" was her sell on this whole life change coming up. Absolutely not, was my attitude. So, I ended up moving in with my dad, whom I hadn't lived with since I was ten years old.

He tried to make things nice. I mean, the home was clean, and he would make my dinner every day before he left, but our schedules were different so while I was at school, he was home and when I was home, he was at work. This made for plenty of time to get high and have my boyfriend over. I was only allowed to pick one day of the weekend to spend the night at my bestie's, and boy, would we make up for it. My mom had left me a Dodge dart, as her husband's family had a surplus of cars. This would be my first car. What a nightmare. My mom would send me letters telling me how much fun they were having and how much she missed me and wished I was there.

I didn't realize it at the time, but man, was my bag of resentments getting filled to the brim. I do love my parents for being good people at heart, but the generational curse of not thinking things through was in full swing. My mom ended up moving back home by my senior year and I moved back in with her. By then though, the drugs and dysfunction had become a part of my world.

So here we were, in our second nice home, with my mom leaving the scene again. It didn't matter to me, my love affair with the vodka bottle was trying to hide from her anyway. It wouldn't be long before I'd grow acclimated to the sounds and surroundings every single mother must tune into to get a good night's sleep. I would take the kids to the pool often. I taught the boys how to swim and they were little fish. We'd swim and laugh and all the while, my drinking was constant.

My next-door neighbor was a guy who was nine years younger than me. Ike was renting a room from a friend, and they had become familiar with me and my chaos. 'The lady next door with all the kids who yells quite frequently' is what they thought, I'm sure. But this guy also lived with his girlfriend. He would come over and smoke weed, and we got to know each other quite well. One day he asked me to give him a ride to get some weed and I had just showered and had no makeup on. I didn't wear much makeup back in those days, I wasn't going anywhere. The liquor store didn't care what I looked like. I had been up for a couple of days, and I remember asking him if I looked okay. "What, with your natural beauty?" was his reply. Couldn't he see it? Did he have no clue that half of our conversations took place with me highly under the influence? Either way, our relationship grew, and he became one of my dearest friends. He's still a dear friend to this day. He loved the kids, and let's face it, who didn't? By the grace of God, I was blessed with some really great kids. I had a lot going for me in my normal state, but the fear of success, mixed in with the load of baggage I was carrying around with a tight grip, wouldn't allow for that part of me to come out. By this time, Jack's lack of involvement with the kids was at an all-time high. Today I can look back and see the missed opportunities for setting firm boundaries, but it all made me who I am today.

The boys were in baseball, my daughter had a few friends, and things were going along somewhat okay. I was a mess. The drinking was daily, from the time I got up until whenever I'd finally slow down enough to rest. There were a few times that Jack would have the kids for the weekend. I would drive them up to meet him and would be so excited for them to see him. After dropping them off, I'd stop and pick up a burrito and a bottle. I'd go home, open the sofa sleeper in the living room, and grab a couple of VHS movies that I loved. Ike would come over and ask, "Why do you always watch your eighties movies when the kids are gone?" It was comfortable; I thought of it as recharging my batteries. I wasn't recharging, I was going around the same mountain, over and over again.

Due to being on State aid, I had to meet my worker at times. Another huge blessing was that I had a worker who adored me. He would ask, "What can I do to help? How can we get you to stop drinking?" One time, he thought he'd found an answer. He left the room and came back with a form. He was so excited. He said, "Here; if you sign this, it will grant you permanent disability due to your alcoholism." I was stunned. I said, "Then I won't be able to work anymore?" He said, "You won't have to. You'll be disabled." I couldn't believe it. "But I want to work, I just can't right now." Mr. Upas was so good to me. He truly cared and was trying to do his job and help me at the same time. I was even offered a no-pay position with the County. I did this for several weeks, but it was interfering with my love affair. Nothing came before my love affair. I decided to enroll in a program that offered case management to me. Who would've known years later that I would work for this same department and be able to read the notes on my file? Oh, the irony.

I did some outpatient treatment while living in this condo. I had been attending for a couple of months and my counselor terrified me. She was good at her job and was starting to figure me out. I didn't want anyone getting to know me that well. I didn't even know myself. But she was not shy about putting into words what was so evident and true. I'd explain to her that after going to a meeting I would buy a bottle, take it home, and stare at it. She said, "Wow, you really do have a relationship with this bottle." I would chintz on the words I used around her; she was getting too close.

Within a month or two, my dad, who had moved to Vegas several years prior—another abandonment—had gotten in a serious car accident. Drunk driving, of course. My mom, who always seemed to be in town rather than traveling, was able to watch the kids, and my sister and I were going to drive to Vegas. By this time, I had maybe two months sober and was still attending the women's outpatient. My sister was still using meth. She and I had, and still have, a rocky relationship, to say the least. We want to love each other, but there's so much baggage that remains. So, we just do holidays and stuff with all this baggage stuffed under a very bumpy rug.

Knowing I had at least a six-hour drive with her, I bought two bottles of vodka for the drive. It was going to be a long ride, let alone what we'd find once we arrived at the hospital in Vegas. Anything I had been striving for went straight out the window. When we arrived, they had put my dad in a coma for the brain swelling to go down. We went back to my dad's and would return to the hospital each day. My sister was also a gambler. I didn't care what she was doing; there was a stocked bar in my dad's house. By the third day or so, with all the emotion swirling around as my dad progressed slowly, I too, ended up doing some meth with my sister.

It was a great excuse to pick right back up in my disease. No one was paying attention and the focus was on my dad. He was able to go home within five days or so and we were going to head back home. All of us thought he would have long-lasting effects from this accident, but he recovered quickly and went on with his life.

Once home, I knew I'd have to go back to my outpatient and act like nothing had happened. It wasn't the alcohol I was worried about; it was the meth in my system. So, I put my return off for a couple of days. My counselor had called and informed me that if I didn't return they'd have to discharge me for lack of attendance. I mustered up the courage I had and went back to face the music. As per protocol, they tested me and I, in fact, came back positive for meth and alcohol. In thinking back, my counselor really did try to walk me through this relapse, but there was a catch. Somehow, I found out that my mom had called and spoken with my counselor. Maybe things were different back then when it came to releasing information, or maybe I'd put my mom as an emergency contact; I'm not sure. But I felt so betrayed that my counselor told my mom any of the confidential things I'd shared with her. Today I know that I used this as another perfect excuse to stop attending treatment.

I hope I'm not losing you in this whole treatment saga. My hope is that as you follow the sequence of events, you'll see that we addicts can come up with any excuse not to face the true issues. What I've learned from my personal experience, and now my professional experience, is that the disease has got to run its course. It's crazy sad for all those involved, but it's an unfortunate fact.

Another side note about this past outpatient treatment, and the counselor I was terrified of, was that in the coming years, she would end up being one of my teachers when I started to attend addiction counseling school. And then another few years later, she ended up being a co-worker.

It really is a small world and if you've read this far, as I've mentioned, my hope is that whatever stage you're at in your journey, you'll be able to see that all your stories and events had to happen just as they did. They're all pieces to our puzzle in the journey of life. This goes for everyone, even those who've never dealt with any addiction. The goal is to enjoy the journey; there is no destination to arrive at.

While attempting to pick up the pieces and continue on with life, it didn't really bother me that at this point, I'd been through five treatment episodes. As with all things in life, you pick up what you can use and leave the rest. By this time in my drinking career, the vodka was starting to take a toll on my body. I would have times when nothing stayed down except vodka. There was one summer that I stayed in my little bathing suit that doubled as a dress because I was internally on fire. I was also drinking and driving a lot. I mean, my Blood Alcohol Content had to have been up to a .20 on a daily basis. That is no exaggeration.

It was around this time that my landlord informed me that she was getting a divorce and would be selling the condo. I think we'd been in this place for two and a half years, but it was time to move again.

This time I found a nice little house directly across from the elementary school that the boys went to, and it seemed like a perfect fit. The boys would be close to school, my daughter's bus stop was nearby, and the baseball field where the boys played on a team was directly across from the front yard.

CHAPTER *10*

The Tables Turning

It was at this point that my daughter was fed up with my drinking. She had hit puberty at the time I was hitting bottom and an invisible clash was taking place. She had become really vocal about my drinking while in the condo. I had developed a few quirks that we can laugh about today, but how scary for my children.

One of my quirks was that I always let my right hand hang when I was drinking. The kids didn't know why, but they knew this was a sign of my being under the influence. The reason it would hang was because I spent most of the day with a drink in my hand. So, when I was trying to play it off around the kids, without a drink, my hand would naturally hang due to being empty. It was a dead giveaway.

Another quirk I had developed was the slurring of my words. I was always trying to act normal, so I had no idea how much the alcohol was impairing me. My precious daughter would get home from school and yell, "Have you been drinking again?" Appalled, I would answer, "No, of course not; why do you keep asking me that?" She'd say, "You keep talking like you have a feather in your mouth." This became a thing in our house. When Gramma would call, she'd ask, "Is your mom talking with feathers in her mouth?" What a nightmare. I thought, if everybody would get off my ass, maybe I could think straight.

It was at this point that my daughter approached me about wanting to move to North County to live with her dad. He was not very involved in their lives, and he and his girlfriend were still using meth. She wanted to go live with him and go to school up there. The school she had been attending the last few years was a school for performing arts and she had no interest in becoming a ballerina. I knew this was a terrible move, due to the surrounding environment I knew he lived in. But I guess to her, anywhere would've been better than dealing with my drinking.

After much thought and consideration, I still wanted to say absolutely not. She wasn't having it. She'd been very vocal and demanding since she was old enough to talk. The apple never falls far from the tree. Against my better judgment, I allowed this to happen. She packed her things and was off to live forty miles away at her dad's house.

I'll never forget the morning after my daughter moved. It was a Monday and should've been the start of a new week. The boys had school and I should've focused on that. I remember that morning like it was yesterday. When I woke up, the house felt so empty. She wasn't there and the boys were sleeping. How had it come to this? I'd ask myself this same question many times over my years of bondage. I went to the living room and cried for what seemed like an hour. It wasn't a great way to start a new week, but this would be my new normal. I had changed my whole life for this little girl, and nothing mattered to me more than my children.

I couldn't get past the defeat. The only way to numb the feelings that were tearing me apart was, of course, the alcohol. I would try to play it off like it was all going to be fine, but I knew that things had really taken a turn for the worse.

I was hopeful that maybe Jack would become more involved with the boys. I was hopeful that maybe my daughter and I could start rebuilding part of the bond we'd lost due to my dysfunctional life. None of that happened. Now she was coming to visit me on the weekends and wouldn't think twice about leaving after the visit.

Ike was around a lot. He had broken up with his girlfriend and needed a place to stay. He was one of the most 'normal' people I knew and it felt comforting to have him around. I had mentioned that he didn't notice how much I was under the influence in the earlier days. This too, had changed. He was frustrated with my drinking and would express it, often. He would ask, "Why can't you just stop? You're drinking every day. Don't you have other things you'd rather be doing?" I couldn't answer any of these questions. The vodka had me crippled by this point. Nobody's opinion mattered to me at that point, or so I told myself.

It always struck me as odd that the teachers at the boys' school would ask me to work a booth at the Halloween carnival or other events. The boy's baseball coach would ask me to keep stats during the games. When I'd ask Jack how come he wouldn't check on his children, his reply was always, "They're with you; I know they're fine." They weren't fine, I wasn't fine, nothing was fine.

The months rolled on and living without my daughter became the new normal. The whole family worrying about my drinking and "how I was doing" became the new normal. There was even a time when a cop followed me back to my driveway to inform me that I had a taillight out. Even they didn't see a problem with my appearance. It was a façade that I would bank on for a few more years.

During this time, with nothing but time on my hands while the kids were at school, the small community baseball league the boys played in was in dire need of funds to continue to operate. There was a radio station that was giving away a thousand dollars once a week, but you had to log in at ten a.m. on Friday to enter to win. We didn't have a computer or the internet. We didn't have much other than food and a roof over our heads. Any extra money was spent funding the local liquor stores. I had decided to try and help, and so I went to the library to enter the Little League in this contest. The rules were that you had to log on at exactly 10:00 a.m. I had gotten to the library around 9:15 a.m. to be sure I was set up to go when the time came. I had a few minutes to spare and back in those days, the newest thing was the Amber Alerts for sexual predators in your neighborhood. I decided to check it out while waiting for the contest to begin. Tons of red dots showed up on this map and I did a little digging to see if I was familiar with any of these houses or people. One of the ones that stood out was a house right up around the corner. I had seen this man in the neighborhood and knew that he lived there with his wife.

One day, while the boys were at baseball practice across the street, I was cleaning the house and watching them from our front window. I looked up and saw the man who was on this sexual predator list, squatting between third base and home plate. I dropped my broom and headed across the street. I stood and stared at him and asked him which child was his. He said he didn't have a kid on the field, and I took a seat in the bleachers. I thought I'd just sit and monitor this and that way he'd get the hint that someone was onto him. My intentions were never to start a ruckus, but sometimes it ended up that way.

A couple of weeks later, the boys had an early morning game. It was always so great to walk literally across the street and watch the boys play. After the game, we went home and they changed their clothes and asked to go watch the other games going on. This was fine as I would be right there in the living room watching TV, and drinking.

After a while, I looked out and noticed this same man sitting in the bleachers. I stormed over there and was so offended that he had the nerve to be there. I shouted at him, "Why are you here? You need to leave." Some young guy jumped up from the bleachers, towering over me by a foot, and yelled, "Hey man, that's my dad you're talking to." "Yes, well, your dad is on the neighborhood sex offender list and has no business being here." My poor boys were humiliated. One of the baseball moms came out of the snack shack and gently asked me to go home. I took the boys and stormed off. I was furious that people could be so blatant in their behavior.

The following baseball practice, the league ended up thanking me. They had no idea that these predators were lurking around and appreciated that someone was paying attention. We never won the contest to help the league stay open. It became a very quiet baseball field that would only be used occasionally by the elementary school. This was the same baseball field/park where the chains were broken for me several years later.

When I talk about the tables turning, it was certainly at this point where my daily routine was to attempt to function through the day, while I was drinking. At night, once the boys were bathed and in bed, I would listen to music. I was always well aware of the mess I was in and the extent of my problem. I would cry out to God and ask Him to give me a vision, to help me find my way out of this mess. I knew in my heart that all the blessings I had around me were becoming a crutch for me. The Section 8 housing, the worker who would tolerate and sympathize with my drinking, and my family who was watching from the sidelines unaware of how to help. My bondage had me exactly where it wanted me. Straight stuck.

My attempts to function were ongoing and I'd set up a pool in the backyard, hang sheets out to dry, and prune the beautiful yellow rose bushes in front of the house, but the chaos continued. I don't think I went to treatment while living in that house. My mom and I had such a strained relationship by this time, she was trying to avoid my mess and engage in her plan of traveling. There were times when she'd come into town, but our visits always ended with another blowout.

52

CHAPTER *11*

The Friends I Had

During these years, I had met a lady named Nancy. She was my drinking partner. Nancy had a young adult daughter who had Down syndrome and whom she cared for 24/7. Nancy also didn't have a car. Each morning, after getting the boys across the street to school, I'd head to Nancy's. We'd be the first ones at the liquor store to get our morning bottle. There were days when we'd go to the grocery store after a couple of drinks or the occasional doctor's appointment for her daughter. I'd be back home by noonish and continue to 'play' mom while waiting for the boys to get out of school. My kids knew I was doing this routine and they called her "Poison." They'd ask, "Are you going to Poison's house again?" "She's a nice lady," I'd try to convince them. It didn't matter if she was nice or not, they knew what awaited them when they returned home from school if I'd been hanging out with Nancy.

What they didn't grasp was that the condition I would be in by the time they got home would've been the same, with or without Nancy.

I also had my old man friend, Ronnie, who absolutely adored me. He lived up around the corner too and he had years of wisdom and knowledge that he'd share with me. He, too, was an alcoholic. His past experience had taught him that hard drugs were bad, but that alcohol was a daily part of life. We'd drink and talk, and he would've done anything to protect me. He wasn't too mobile though due to his drinking, and that was fine with me. In my scattered state of mind, this worked perfectly to just go visit, and not have people at my house.

Ronnie would always tell me how much he believed in me and that I could do so much more with my life. He's one of my angels today, as the alcohol killed him within a few short years of knowing him.

Then, of course, I had the random dudes who for some reason, loved to be around me. I kept them to a minimum because I was still trying to live the façade of being a decent mother.

Within a year and a half of living in this home, my landlord informed me that they were getting a divorce and they would be selling the house. Looking for another place seemed to be something I was getting better at. There was a young guy who had come by with another friend one day. He was infatuated with me but much younger than me. He lived up around the corner and he was never anybody I wanted in our life. Through all these years, even through my darkest times, the safety of my children in our homes was always a top priority for me.

I found a house for rent and scheduled an appointment to go look at it. It was up around the corner. When I pulled up to look at it, that same young guy ran outside and yelled, "You can't park here." It was next door to his house, where he lived with his parents. I smiled and said, "I'm looking at the house for rent." The look on his face was dread, but I didn't care. He mattered none to me.

The people who owned this house were so nice. This house was beautiful too. Huge backyard and a big, detached garage, and it was right around the corner from the school. This would be perfect for us, and we put the paperwork in to be approved by Section 8. This would also be the home where it all unraveled.

By this time, Ronnie had sold his childhood home and moved to Arizona. It wasn't long before he drank himself to death. Although he was a severe alcoholic, he was one friend who would keep me grounded and hold me accountable to not indulge in the grime of that lifestyle. He was an angel both alive and deceased.

I had locked in several people in the neighborhood who all served a different purpose. Jerry, Ronnie's next-door neighbor, was also a drinking buddy. He and Nancy would hang out at

Ronnie's house hours after I'd be home with the kids. I was also closer to my first and most frequented liquor store. Basically, this last place we lived was two blocks behind the first home we lived in. Oh, how different I was from when, just several years earlier, I had walked in there for the first time with the boys in a double stroller. The alcohol was ravaging my body, heart, and soul.

And, of course, my new next-door neighbor, to the other side of me, was a lonely old guy, who drank and smoked weed. He was a grumpy old man, but he would laugh and smile with me. He too loved loud music and would welcome any time I'd spare to hang out with him.

The tone was set. Keep the kids in school and drink with whoever was available. I actually drank even when there wasn't a social scene of any kind going on. That's all I did. Nothing happened in my world until I had a few drinks in me. I've always been an early riser and by this time, I was drinking straight vodka at five a.m. There were mornings when I was shaking so badly I'd have to stick a straw in the vodka bottle to get a few sips in me. There were days when the boys would say, "Oh Mom I forgot; can you sign this form?" I would panic because my hand was so unsteady I couldn't even write my name.

I'm not sure if I had gone to detox during the last two houses we lived at. I may have, but there certainly isn't a time that stood out in my mind. All of my treatment experiences have at least one or two vivid memories attached to them.

We were just existing. At this point, my mom would call throughout the week and get the boys on the phone. She'd ask them about school and baseball, but what they'd really talk about was me and my drinking. Today I know that my oldest son, who was only eight years old at the time, would tell Gramma about 'marking' my bottles. He would tell her, "I drew a line so I can tell how much she drank." My mom would encourage him not to and informed him that I probably had several bottles hidden. She was right.

There was a time when I took the recyclables up around the corner. The little Hispanic lady there was so nice. The plastic soda bottles and the aluminum can baskets were quite empty. But the glass container was two feet full. She asked me, "Oh, *m'ija*, did you drink all this?" "No, of course not, I have a lot of friends that come over and hang out with me." All lies. I never took those to be recycled again. I'd do the bottle sweep two or three times per week when the boys were in school. Empty pints or fifths of vodka tucked under a sweater, in the unused lingerie drawer, in the file cabinet under useless paper, in the closet in a shoe box, wherever I'd remember I put it, but out of sight. Every week on trash day, in this quiet little neighborhood, the recycle bin could be heard for blocks. The clanging of the multiple bottles was so loud. I'd always be so grateful when they were done with our block.

It was at this house that so many signs were there. Signs of deep trouble on the horizon. My family was terribly worried about me. My daughter would only come to visit but never stay longer than one or two nights. She'd come to visit the boys but would exit as quickly as she could due to having to deal with me. The boys were coming home to a mother who was passed out at least one day a week. We had two little dogs. One of them, a chihuahua, had belonged to the roommate of Ike at the condos. She would wander under the cracked garage door and come up the stairs to see the boys. Although there was a storm brewing in every house we lived in, the kids were full of life and love. When Ike's roommate was moving back to New Jersey, he asked if we wanted to keep her. Gypsy was her name, and she was a smart and loyal girl. If that dog could talk, I would've been in jail. There were days when, after taking the boys to school, I'd do my usual swing by the liquor store, and Gypsy would jump out the window and come in the store looking for me. I'd bring the bottle home and Gypsy would stare and sigh. She knew this was going to be bad. There had been a litter of Chihuahua/Dachshund mix puppies born at my daughter's boyfriend's house up north. I got one and gave it to my son for his birthday in December 2006. Tank and Gypsy, they were the only two that would hang out with me, day in and day out. We had hardwood floors and all day, as I'd walk around and attempt to keep things in order, their little feet would tap, tap, tap behind me. It was a mess.

About a year into living at her dad's house, my daughter realized that he and his girlfriend were as big of a mess, if not more, than I was. Just meth instead of alcohol. She had made a couple of friends up there and had a boyfriend. She had transitioned into living at her boyfriend's family's house. They were nice and she felt safer there. Coming back home was not an option she would even consider. She was in a charter school to complete her high school credits and was working at a coffee shop. She had learned, with little help from either parent, how to eat healthy and take care of herself, by the age of sixteen.

So much happened in this house. Aside from the little punk that lived next door trying to dictate who came and went from my house, I was at an all-time high of having absolutely nothing in order. Sure, the house looked clean, most of the time, but I was serving my kids crappy meals, trying to dodge any contact with my mom, and stashing away every penny that came in for my next bottle.

My landlord was a nice Hispanic man. He and his wife had a toddler, and they managed some big senior complex a few miles away. Since this home was the first property they owned, he wanted to be the one who did the lawn. He would come twice a month and mow and edge the yard. He was always very nice to me and a few months after living there, even he expressed some concern about me being sick, or how I was doing. I had set up a badminton net in the backyard and he would always ask to play a game with me. Seemed odd, but anything that appeared to be normal, I would engage in. To an outsider, I may have seemed fine. Between the teachers still asking me to volunteer at school and my landlord wanting to play games with me, I'm not sure what they thought about me. Today I know that it was God's light in me, fighting to blossom and flourish.

CHAPTER *12*

Thanksgiving 2005

*M*y mom and stepdad had sold their home a few years prior and were supposed to be traveling. And, though they did some traveling, it seemed as if they were in town more often than not. When they were coming to town, my mom would call a week or two before their arrival and give me their agenda and how this was going to happen, and they were going to pick up the kids for this or that. These weeks leading up to their arrival were always a stressful time for me. I wanted to be able to enjoy their visits and the kids loved being with Gramma. But I knew that my mom's agenda always included a complete survey of what and how I was doing, with my drinking. There was so much pressure to have a "good report," and this just made me drink even more.

This particular Thanksgiving was going to be a good one. They had taken the kids for a few days before the holiday and would be bringing them home on Thanksgiving. I had asked if I could make the dinner so that when they arrived we could eat as a family. All was approved and I looked forward to the family meal. That morning, I was excited that I was able to get up and prepare a meal for us to enjoy. I took careful steps to ensure my drinking wouldn't get out of control that day. I cleaned the house and got things in order. I enjoyed preparing the meal and all was in place. They were to arrive by noon or one p.m. As the day went on, the time of arrival came and went. Another hour went by, and all was still well. Three hours past the scheduled time of arrival, I consumed a bit more alcohol. By the time they arrived, it was way past four p.m. and I was now scrambling to keep the food hot and ready. I also had let the circumstances get to me a bit more than necessary. When they arrived, my mom came in and started yelling at me that they weren't staying. In her words, "You've been drinking, and we're taking the boys." The boys, so over confrontation, went back to the car. As I went to retrieve them, my stepdad came to my side gate and got in my face. I didn't hesitate, and a fistfight ensued between him and me. I was so furious! And off they drove. Another attempt to be a good mom – failed! Abandonment, anger, bitterness...they always seemed to be the highlight of my events.

CHAPTER *13*

Gasping for Air

*W*e didn't live there longer than a year and a half and these next few stories all happened in that short amount of time. This was also the season of my drinking when the cops were starting to filter in.

I had mentioned I had several drinking buddies who lived within close proximity to us. One day, while the kids were at school, I had gone to see Joe and Tracy. I was a mess. We had done some meth, but the vodka was always most prevalent. They dropped me off at my house around noon so I could prepare for the kids' arrival after school. My friends must've known the condition I was in because they walked me to my back door. I don't really remember this happening, but I'll never forget their reaction. As I attempted to unlock the back door, I fell straight over and landed the three steps down. Of course, I didn't feel a thing. My friends got me into my room and told me to take a nap.

I was only asleep for a little while and kept hearing the doorbell and the dogs barking. I got up to go answer the door and there were cops standing there. I was in a blackout so I was not too concerned about them being there. I unlocked the door, told them I was napping, and to go ahead and look around. They didn't stay long, and I don't know who had sent them. I just remember the lady cop telling me to finish my nap and to call them if I needed anything.

To the average person this would've been a huge wake-up call, but I was in such bondage to the vodka. I wrote it off as some annoyance and was offended that they were even checking on me. The next day, Joe and Tracy came to check on me, too. Of course, I woke up with a few bruises from the fall, but I was determined to stay alert and not let these circumstances get the best of me.

Soon thereafter, it was football season, and I was keeping up the facade of being a good mom. One Sunday, I asked the boys what snacks they would want for the game. It was a perfect excuse to make a store run. I picked up their snacks and of course, more vodka. All these memories are so vivid to me, even to this day.

As we watched the game, and I monitored my drinking, I thought things were going fine. I also had a routine of taking several short showers each day. First would be the five a.m. shower, so I could look presentable for my six a.m. liquor store run. Then, throughout the day, I'd "rinse off," mostly to wake up a little, and it always gave me a burst of energy. During the game, the boys were on the phone with their sister. She'd call to check on them and spend very little time talking to me. When the game ended, I jumped in the shower to ready myself for the evening.

When I walked out of the shower, with one towel on my head and another around my body, there were cops standing in my living room. I couldn't believe it. My daughter had called the cops and the boys had let them in. Appalled, I asked if I could at least get dressed. They allowed that. I threw on some shorts and a sweatshirt and came to the living room to discuss the reason for their visit. My goal each day, due to all the blackout days prior, was to monitor my alcohol intake and not get in any trouble. This day was no different and I specifically remember only buying a half pint, so I wouldn't drink too much.

They had the boys in their room and were advising me that they were old enough to decide if they wanted to stay or leave. I believe the boys were being persuaded by their sister to leave, which they chose to do, but what they didn't know was that it would be twenty-four hours before my mom could come to their rescue. So, there they went. Backpack on one shoulder and skateboard in their other hand. I couldn't believe the turn of events. They had been safe with me. They'd had a somewhat normal day. We'd only been watching the Chargers game.

My opinion didn't matter anymore. The dirt was becoming evident and the world around me was watching.

I sat there crying, as usual, and wondering how I could fix this. There was only one way to fix any of it, and that would be to stop drinking. The alcohol was nowhere near done with me. My boys spent the night at the child protection center. My mom came to get them the next day and took them back up to Borrego Springs, where her motor home was docked at that time.

Next came the weeks of trying to get the kids back home. One of the biggest resentments I had built against my mother was how she was always trying to stick her nose where it didn't belong. "The kids need to be in school," I'd say. "I've already talked to the school and they're sending their work to me," was her reply. I couldn't believe it. For years my mom hadn't hugged me without taking a huge inhale to see if I'd been drinking. She was still so wounded from growing up with alcoholic parents and marrying a functional alcoholic. But I was her daughter. Hadn't she abandoned me enough times to know how much I needed her support rather than her criticism?

My plan was to drive to Borrego Springs and pick up the boys. There was just one glitch that no amount of sobriety or determination was going to get past and that was the fact that they were on a military base. I couldn't get through the gate without permission, and they didn't give me permission.

I spent the next week downtown at the family law building trying to get some answers about my rights. Again, another angel had been put in my life. I left no part of the story out and there was the nicest lady there who really helped me. She gave me all the scenarios, but the main point was that unless my mom had any custody rights, the boys needed to be returned to me.

Another Thanksgiving rolled around during the three weeks that my mom had the boys. I bought one of those prepared meals from Vons and ate by myself. It was all crashing down on me and I was determined to make things better.

I informed my mom of the family law and what kind of trouble she'd be in if she didn't bring the boys back. Reluctantly, she returned them. She and I weren't really speaking at this time and my stepdad, and I still didn't care to even see each other.

The next several months were spent on pins and needles. I felt so alone and knew that everybody was just waiting for me to screw up. I'd sit in my room, night after night, trying to figure out how I could get out of this lifestyle. I knew that Section 8 had become a crutch to leading a more productive life. And although I cherished the workers in my life who were sympathetic to my disease, I knew this too, was only coddling my disease.

I watched myself very closely for the next few months and gave it a Girl Scout effort to be a good mother. The drinking hadn't stopped, not even close. I was just more careful about what I did and who would be there to witness any of it. The boys and the dogs all walked on eggshells around me.

The next big disaster would be running into Charlie, the guy I had met when my daughter was only three years old. One day, after taking the boys to school, I picked up Nancy and we headed to the liquor store. She lived in a trailer park and as we pulled into the park after our liquor store run, the lady who lived in the first trailer in the park was outside and flagged Nancy down. We stopped long enough for this lady to tell us that she'd had a snake in her house and how thankful she was that these two guys had gotten it out for her. From around her backyard came two men. It was at first glance that I recognized that walk. It was Charlie.

Charlie was a die-hard dope fiend. He was crazy in the most fun-loving way a dope fiend could be. He was also a sociopath. I put the car in park and hopped out. I couldn't believe it, after all these years I'd run into someone who I'd always loved. Today I know it was my disease that loved him. I could be dysfunctional around him, and he'd always allow it because he never had any intention of making his life better.

Come to find out, Charlie lived just down the way from Nancy. It was just like running into Brad, a hope for me that someone who knew me back in my younger years would now be in my life and in my corner. Charlie and I hugged and exchanged phone numbers. It didn't take long before Charlie had filtered back in and yet another toxic person would be there in the midst of my mess.

Charlie had asked if I wanted to go out to dinner. He said, "But you can't be drunk when we go." So, I got ready and didn't drink. When he picked me up, I was shaking so bad from not drinking, he couldn't believe it. He allowed me to have a sip and thought he could fix me in some way. I should've known that this too would lead to disaster, but I was grasping for any kind of help.

One of the stipulations to living in these beautiful homes was that I paid the water bill. This seemed doable and probably would have been had I not been spending every penny on alcohol. The water had been shut off twice while living in this home. Both times I called the water company and told them that the bill had been paid, and like magic, the guy would come and turn it back on. I would work on paying it as the weeks went by.

The third time this happened was on May 31, 2007, my birthday. I called the water company and informed them that the bill had been paid, but they weren't buying it. They said they'd need confirmation and that the water would stay off until they had proof. I was in a panic. I couldn't let the boys come home and not have running water.

My plan was to pack a bag for us and spend the night at Nancy's. I knew the boys wouldn't be thrilled with this but at least they could shower and flush the toilet. I was crushed, and when I was in over my head, I'd drink too much.

The boys came home from school, and I informed them that we were going to Nancy's for the night. They bitched and moaned, and I tried to make it seem like it was all going to be okay. Nancy's house was only a mile away if that, and then the half mile into the trailer park. I put the boys in the car, drove to Nancy's, and that's all I remember. The next thing I knew I was laying on Nancy's couch. When I woke up I did the all-too-familiar panic of, *Where are the boys?* Nancy asked me if I was okay. "Where are the boys?" I asked.

Nancy explained to me that once I parked in her driveway, one foot out the driver's door, I had passed out. The boys, who had met Charlie within the past few weeks and knew which trailer was his, had gotten out of the car and walked to his house. He brought them down to check on me, but I wasn't budging. I was beyond drunk and couldn't even get myself out of the car.

He took them back home and they called Gramma. My mom was out in Borrego Springs, so she sent my sister to get them from Charlie.

Sitting in Nancy's house, completely defeated, I knew this would be the last straw. Of course, I reached for my bottle, it was the only thing that was going to keep me from losing my mind. I can't remember if I called my mom or not, but there was no way of talking my way out of this one.

I'd go back and forth from my house to Nancy's for the next few days and just wallow in the mess I'd made. Although Nancy felt terrible for me, there was nothing she could do. She was always a good friend to me, no matter the circumstances. As for Charlie, he was appalled at my behavior, but this would be the platform he'd use in the coming years to anchor his toxicity on me.

June 5, 2007, I got a call from my dad, at Nancy's house. All completely odd considering my dad had no idea where I was or who I hung out with. He knew there was a problem with my drinking; the whole family knew. He nonchalantly asked me how I was and then reminded me I had an appointment at the Social Services office the next day. "I do?" was my response. He went on to say "Yes, I just wanted to remind you. How about I pick you up, we can have lunch, and I'll take you to your appointment." It sounded great. All I ever needed was my family to check on me, to truly care about me, and not judge me. I mean, after all, it was through generations, on both sides, that this alcoholic gene had been given to me.

I didn't think anything of it. I agreed to meet my dad at my house at eleven a.m. I obviously hadn't thought it through. I couldn't tell my head from my ass at this point, so any guidance was gladly welcomed.

Back then, I had these little jean skorts I would wear often. They were cute and cozy and perfect for flitting around in a drunken stupor. I showered at Nancy's that morning, threw on my clothes, and headed to my house to meet my dad. When he picked me up he was horrified at my condition but played it off as if he was a concerned parent. We went to Jack in the Box and sat inside and ate. Small talk was had, and I asked how he knew about this appointment. He said my mom had informed him and I just thought, Hmm?

When we arrived at the office, we walked in and up to the window to check in. Within a few minutes they came to get me, and my dad stood up to follow me. I said, "I'll be right back," but he insisted that he go too. We walked down the hall and into a room and BOOM, there they were. My whole family! My mom and my stepdad, my sister, my daughter, my bestie, my sister-in-law, and three social workers, two of whom were from the CPS department. They had the tables in a U-shape, and they were all sitting around staring at me. I was blown away by their deception and interference. I chose a seat next to my daughter, laid my head on her shoulder, and sobbed. After all the abandonment and half-assed love they'd given over the years, how dare they do this to me?

I was drunk. I kept asking where the hidden cameras were, this had to be a joke. The social workers asked everyone to write their names on foldable paper so they could address them during this meeting. "Just so you know, I'm keeping all these names for my scrapbook when we're done," was a comment I made. The time had come to truly face the music. Nothing I said was going to matter at this point. They continued with their plan. It was my decision to either allow my mom to have temporary custody of the boys or the State would get involved and do what they needed to keep the boys safe.

"I'm not signing over custody of my kids to you; you raised me and look how screwed up I turned out." My bestie chimed in that my mom didn't want to be raising my kids, but it was best for the boys if I allowed my mom to take them.

I cried and cried and couldn't even fathom what was happening. Where were all these people in the years leading up to this? All they would have had to do was to sincerely be concerned and maybe things would've been different. Who knows? Today I know that all of this had to happen exactly as it did for the chains to be broken.

They explained to me that they already had a spot for me at detox and that in order for the boys to return to me, I needed to have at least six months clean. My only two options were to comply with their plan or to walk away from my kids. All I ever wanted to do was be a good mom and show my kids how much I loved them.

For the next hour or so, they sorted out the specifics, and how the boys would be cared for. I was furious and heartbroken. My precious daughter—what a strong woman she has always been, even at such a young age—let me cry on her shoulder the entire time. Today, I know that I too, am and have always been, a strong woman, who was clouded by the bondage of bitterness and substances.

It was probably two p.m. by this time, and I hadn't had a drink in a few hours. We had to wait for the clinic around the corner to return from lunch to pick up a prescription for Librium to take to detox. It wasn't my first time with the Librium. This is a medicine that will help the detoxing alcoholic not have a seizure. As I sat in my dad's truck, he was frantic. I was shaking by this point due to needing a drink. My bestie came to the window with a Snickers bar and a Dr. Pepper and said, "Nin, look what I brought you." I was sitting on my hands to keep from shaking and I just smiled at her. They had no clue how bad my body was ravished from the alcohol. I knew. And I knew this was only the beginning of a very long road ahead.

My whole afternoon was suddenly taking a turn I could've never seen coming. The Librium was only to be opened and dispensed by the detox staff. I said my goodbyes to my family and was dropped off at detox and they assured me they'd bring me some clothes. I hobbled up the two flights of stairs to the detox unit and they told me to have a seat in the living room. I was asking about the Librium, of course. There were many emotions going on in my head, mostly the feeling of dread.

Detox wasn't so bad. I knew I was safe, and I knew my family was happy that I was taking a step in the right direction. After a couple of days, with the help of the medicine, I started to feel a bit stronger. I completed detox and was scheduled to go into a residential treatment. There was a glitch in the availability, so I had to return home for a couple of days. By this time, my daughter was in our home more frequently; mostly they were devising a plan on what they'd do with the rental.

I really did intend to stay on the straight and narrow plan until my bed at residential opened up but, as us addicts do, I found some reason to throw a fit and drove to Nancy's. My daughter was so upset. Nancy and I drank for most of the night, and, having learned my lesson about driving in that condition, I slept at her house. One of the stipulations about getting into residential treatment was you had to check in each morning. You guessed it, the following morning they informed me that my bed was ready and to be there by noon.

I drove home and was in a panic about packing my suitcase. I asked my daughter to help me, and she just rolled her eyes at me and said, "No, you figure it out." Hungover and panicked, I crammed what I thought would be appropriate attire into a suitcase, gathered whatever sense I had, and zipped up the suitcase. As soon as I picked it up, the zipper ripped, and all my crap came tumbling out. I didn't care; I'd carry it gently. I got out to my car, and it wouldn't start. Scrambling to make the noon deadline, I ran next door to my neighbor and asked him for a jump. He handed me a handheld battery jumper and said, "Leave it on the porch when you're done."

I got the car started, ran the battery back to his porch, took a deep breath, and headed out to what I thought would be a few months in residential treatment. I parked across the street from this old Victorian house and swooped up my belongings. We did some paperwork and they said, "You'll have to stay in your room for the evening; we can smell alcohol. Didn't you just get out of detox?" I was lucky they even let me stay.

CHAPTER 14

The Long Haul

This was supposed to be a three-month program. I was there for five months. I guess I'm special. During the next few weeks, the paperwork for temporary custody was being finalized and I was ordered to appear at that same family law building where staff had helped me so much a few months earlier.

In this residential program, we weren't allowed to go anywhere alone. We had to take someone with us who'd been in the program longer than us, for support. We weren't allowed to talk to any outsiders and would get written up for doing so. I'm not sure how I can remember each outfit I was wearing during these crucial times, maybe because I always felt like it was me, and God, facing all these trying times.

I leaned against this brick wall of the building, in white capris and a little black sweater, just crying. The paperwork had been sent to me prior, and reading about my mess on paper was just heart-wrenching. I knew it was that bad. Actually, I knew it was worse. The paperwork detailed the many examples of my family having to rescue the boys and multiple dates in the prior years where my family had been concerned for the boys' safety. It was horrible.

My mom and my stepdad came walking up to the building. There wasn't much love or exchange of words, only a deep hurt and betrayal running through me. Waves of memories came rushing back. The years of babysitting after school for my little brother when my mom was at work, my junior year in high school when she up and moved to Germany with my siblings, the years of hugging me while inhaling deeply to check if I'd been drinking, the years of showing up to "save" the kids while leaving me alone. All of it. The size of my baggage had reached an all-time high, or so I thought. Just like the suitcase that ripped on the way out the door, there was still more baggage that had to be crammed in it.

The meeting with the family law people was bone-achingly hard. They tried to make it seem like this would just be temporary until I got some sobriety established. I was crushed, heartbroken, angry, bitter, and sad—very sad. We got through the meeting. Again, no real love was exchanged between my mom and me. They had gotten their way and I was left to walk through this all on my own.

During the next few weeks, I'd see the kids for a two-hour span once a week at the residential treatment program. In this program, the whole day was planned out for you and you either complied or chanced getting kicked out. This was set up to be a behavior modification program. This meant that anything you did wrong, your peers were supposed to inform the staff and once a week, these mistakes were highlighted in a group meeting. Once your mistakes were identified, depending on how many you had that week, you either were ordered to sit on the bench and read the rule book or you'd be put in "exile." There were also the extreme mistakes that called for an "encounter" in a group setting. If you were encountered, the whole facility, staff, and residents would berate you for over an hour to help you see your flaws. Somehow, I managed to make it all five months without ever being encountered. I didn't dare bring it up; I think it was a requirement. Either way, I certainly wasn't going to point it out.

I did spend several hours on the bench reading the rule book for ridiculous things like showering too early or laughing at inappropriate things. They had to do something with every resident to "fix" us. I was also put exile toward the end of my stay for not turning in a paper on time. The paper was nonsense. How was writing a two-page biography going to cover the years of cumulative addiction? Anyway, I was ordered to sit at a side table for two days, all day, and not move until that paper was written.

By my fourth month, I was allowed to go out and get a job. Many of the girls I was in the program with had gotten a job at a famous ice cream parlor. I decided to give it a shot. I was hired, given my apron and hat, and had a start date. The girls I was in treatment with and worked with had become my clique and we would laugh and serve ice cream to the masses. They would always joke about, "I smoked and drank my life away, and now I'm making waffle cones." It took some of the sting out of it but always felt so degrading. I had to have a job to complete the program.

Next, I would move on to a sober living facility and try to build some stability with work, aftercare once a week at the residential facility, and make time to see the kids. All of this was done while using public transportation. Charlie had picked up my car for me a day or two after being in treatment and had it in his driveway. Aside from the fact that I couldn't register it due to it not passing the smog test, I had no desire to get back in that car.

As for our home, I had set up the paperwork for Section 8 to be transferred to my daughter as she was over the age of eighteen. She would've had to find a smaller place, but it was such a gift that was given to me, and I didn't want to lose the voucher. She wanted nothing to do with the paperwork involved in this process and the voucher was lost. They packed up all my stuff and put it in storage. The State, of course, had required them to find a home to live in and not have the boys in the RV.

The boys were in school and playing baseball. When my schedule allowed, I would take the bus and go to their games. Another huge form of embarrassment and bitterness. Very early into joining the soccer moms in the stands, I came to realize that everyone knew my story. My mom had obviously explained, in great detail, the reason she was the caregiver of the boys. This betrayal was shoved in my large tote of baggage, and I would do my best to muster up the courage to sit and smile.

It all felt so overwhelming. The wage at the ice cream parlor certainly wasn't going to be enough to establish my own living quarters again. I would spend the night at my mom's house with the boys occasionally, but every time they dropped me off at the trolley station, my anger and resentment would rise back up. It was getting to the point that just making up excuses to not go see the boys felt better than dealing with all the emotions that came with the visits. Today I know that this was my disease just waiting for me to break.

It was during these five months at this sober living that Charlie infiltrated back into my world. They say it is people, places and things that'll take you back to active addiction, and that part is true. Here I was again, craving any form of normality in my life. I'd go spend the night with Charlie and I could feel the darkness around me. He was absolutely unstable in every way. He swore he wasn't using drugs, but I knew better. I kept telling myself that as long as I didn't pick up a drink, I would be safe.

One day Charlie called after I got back from work, and he was being so nice. Charlie, by nature, was not a nice person. He was telling me that he was cleaning out one of his toolboxes and found some meth. I was highly concerned. I encouraged him to throw it away, flush it, whatever it took to not use it. He said he would. He asked if I wanted to come over, so I did. He picked me up and was all chatty and sweet and I ignored the gut-wrenching dread I felt. When we got to his house, we made small talk for a few minutes and then he flitted off, in his normal form, tinkering on things around the house. He was in his bedroom, so I made my way in. On his bathroom counter were lines of meth. I was startled, scared, and insulted. I wandered around the house, back to the living room, to the backyard to smoke, anywhere I could to get away from this risk.

It didn't take long before I was lingering near the counter. I asked him why he didn't throw it away and why he was putting me in this situation. I could've walked out, but the hook was already in my mouth.

That night I woke up the tiger again. I would continue to tell myself over the next several weeks that as long as I didn't drink, this phase would pass. It wasn't every day that I would use meth, but most times, when with Charlie, there would be the option. I'd also tell myself the biggest lie and that was that nobody would notice.

I completed aftercare from the residential treatment program. I remember sitting in that last meeting, having used meth the day before, just trying to be myself. The girls at my sober living had no idea but they had other issues going on. This particular sober living was a dump. There were men who lived in the back house and women in the front house. Aside from outside boyfriends, most of the girls and guys would all intermingle at all hours of the day. My roommate, who was in her late twenties, was gay and had one child who lived with her parents. She also had mental health issues and wasn't paying attention to anything but her moods. This all worked as a bonus for me.

I never enjoyed using—not in my early years, not in the middle years, and certainly not in those last years. I always felt so guilty and scared. I know today that it was my spirit, my God-given spirit, that I was crushing every time I tried to cover up the pain with substances.

One of the girls I worked with had moved on to another sober living. This sober living was deemed "the place to be." It was a nicer facility and the people in the home were serious about their recovery. I convinced myself that if I could make it there, I could get myself back on track. There came an opening, and I took it. Mind you, moving to another sober living, in my heart, was only going backward from my main goal of making it back home to my children. But I went for it, grasping for any quality of life I could.

By this time, I knew my family was catching on to some of my behaviors. But I didn't smell like alcohol, so they had no proof. It wasn't often that I was using, but it was in my life and that was all it needed. I lived in this second sober living for a couple of months. It had been over a year at this point since the intervention had taken place. The people in this sober living were very serious about their recovery and held each other accountable for their behaviors. I was a compliant resident. I would do my chores, make sure I didn't make any waves, and didn't get too close to anybody emotionally. I was still seeing Charlie and dealing with his erratic behavior.

Around November 2008, just as I had when I walked out of that job years earlier, to save face, I decided I should find another place to live before someone figured out I wasn't completely sober. Charlie had a second bedroom that he had offered to rent to me, and I thought this would be a step in the right direction. He had a son a few years younger than mine. I ran it past my mom, and she absolutely had a fit. I explained to her that at least I could have the boys stay the night with me and that it would be a good transition point. It was anything but!

CHAPTER *15*

Fooling Myself

The first time I tried to have the boys for the night, my mom insisted that I take her car in case they wanted to come home or there was an emergency. It was early afternoon, and we were going to grill some burgers for the boys. Charlie had his son that weekend too. The boys didn't care to talk to each other, let alone play together. I tried to just get through the first hour or two with lighthearted small talk, but they weren't having it. Only minutes after we ate, Charlie yelled from the kitchen, "Hey, are you going to come do these fucking dishes or what?" My boys were terrified. I quickly did the dishes and took the boys in my room. They were so sad. They asked if he always talked to me like that and I explained that he stressed out over little things. Again, they weren't having it. They pondered for a few minutes and said, Take us home. I tried to reason with them that we would be okay; we could just cuddle, and everything would be alright. They were ready to go. I couldn't blame them. My only wish was to have a safe haven to call home, too.

We said our goodbyes and got into my mom's car. I had called my mom to tell her that the boys didn't want to stay. She was fine with that, of course. They all wanted me to stay the night with them, but I told them I couldn't, and they dropped me back off at the trolley station.

I was crushed. Nothing new in my world. Renting that room from Charlie only lasted two months. I knew he was using but hadn't realized until being under the same roof as him that he was actually using meth intravenously. I was in great danger, and I knew it. There came a day during those two months where

Charlie handed me some cash as we pulled up to put gas in his car and he told me to go in and pay. I went into the store, paid for the gas, turned to walk away, and the liquor caught my eye. I stopped in my tracks and thought for a minute. A very short minute. I decided, what could one hard lemonade hurt? As long as it wasn't straight vodka, I'd be fine.

As if the many years prior hadn't taught me a thing, I was right back where I started, in complete bondage. Charlie had no idea I had bought this lemonade. It was in my purse. The same place my bottle would be for the next fourteen and a half months.

In my half-assed attempts to have visits with my kids, I made my way back to the neighborhood I grew up in. My boyfriend from high school and I had remained friends over the years and his family was like family to me. His mom was always a lady I could talk to and feel safe with. It was at this point that she too had a room for rent. I didn't hesitate. I knew with every fiber of my being that being anywhere other than under Charlie's roof would be better for me. I packed up my very few belongings and made my way to my new residence.

Some people in this house used, too. I was still working at the ice cream parlor and would spend some nights with the kids. It hadn't taken long before that hard lemonade turned into vodka. It was the same trick, "I'll just buy the little bottle." How delusional can one person be? Two of the three girls I had been in treatment with, and still worked with, had gone back to using and drinking too. I would go to work, and at the end of my shift, I'd grab a soda with ice before leaving. I'd stop at some market around the corner and grab a bottle. While waiting for the trolley, I'd flip the lid, fill it with vodka, and take the sting out of the reality of what my life had become. Thirty-nine years old, working in an ice cream parlor, using public transportation, and having no hope in sight of being reunified with my children.

For the next several months, my mom was anxious and worried. She could tell I was changing, everybody could. I assured her that I was just stressed from all the running around, but she knew better. I lived with my childhood friend's family for almost eight months. During this time, I would go back to the area that I had lived in with the kids and see all those people

I couldn't seem to pull myself away from. This included Nancy, Charlie, and those other few friends that were spread out within a three-mile radius. I could feel myself being pulled back into the abyss, but I couldn't stop it.

One day when I got to work, the one girl I had been in treatment with who hadn't gone back to using and was now a supervisor, called me into the office. She informed me that they were firing me due to being under the influence. She asked me to sign a paper stating that I was, in fact, under the influence. I was not going to sign anything. I told her she could test me if she wanted and insisted that the alcohol smell was from the night before. All lies. Not signing that paper would work out for me months later, but I was ashamed and guilt-ridden. The next couple of weeks would be a rapid decline in any stability I had.

This would've been around August 2009, and I was in my room one day and had called my mom to check on the kids. Knowing I was in no condition to go and visit them, I made up some lame excuse about not feeling well or something and my mom snapped on me. I'll never forget her words as long as I live. She said, "I know you're drinking again, and probably doing other things, and until you figure out what you're going to do, don't call us." I was in shock. The sting of abandonment and betrayal came rushing back. It didn't take much to feel all those emotions over and over again, they hadn't been dealt with at all.

A few minutes later, while sobbing yet again, I distinctly heard the devil whisper in my ear, "The kids don't need you, you're free to do whatever you want." The spiritual battle was at its peak. I remember laying on the floor, face down, hands and legs spread out and thinking, "That is not true, I don't believe it. Even if the kids don't need me, I need them! I don't want to be anywhere in this world without my children in my life."

Picking myself up, I don't remember if I had a drink with me or if I made another store run. But I did know I needed to go back to detox. I was desperate to do anything that would lead me to the right path again.

I called my daughter and asked if she could take me to the emergency room to pick up the Librium I would need for detox. I think that day I had a panic attack; it could've been withdrawal. Either way, I was in a full-blown spiritual battle and every step was on eggshells. I wasn't going to give up. I would fight for what I wanted or die trying.

Within a few days, I had a bed at the same detox I had just gone to a couple of years back. I don't remember who dropped me off at the pick-up point, but into the detox van I went and was very sure I was making a good choice. The first one in quite a while. When we got to the facility, as protocol, they told me to have a seat in the living room. Relieved to be anywhere but alone with a bottle, I sat for just a minute or two.

Around the corner came my friend James. He said, "What are you doing here?" "James!" I exclaimed! "What are you doing here?" He went on to say that he was a counselor at the facility, and he was happy I was there. James and I knew each other from years earlier when my daughter was two years old. Another friend I knew from a much simpler time in my life. As I mentioned about detox, it always felt like a safe place to be. Plus, I was surrounded by people who were at a low point in their lives, too. And now, as a bonus, I'd get to be around James for the next two weeks. This stay at detox was pretty uneventful other than having James as a counselor. Within a day or three, I was starting to feel somewhat decent and was being a compliant client. Each week the detox crew would go to the laundromat to do all the bedding and such. Here were James and I, folding sheets and laughing about how much better life is when you stay sober. The staff had suggested that I go back into a residential program, but I wasn't going to start that whole cycle again. I assured them that I'd get a sponsor, go to meetings, and would call them if I needed resources.

Upon returning to my residence at my high school boyfriend's family home, it didn't take long before I was walking to the liquor store again. At this point, his mom wanted no drama in her house and told me it was time to move on.

I took my belongings and headed out to the area where all my drinking and using buddies lived. I didn't have a set place to live but had several different stops I'd make and was welcomed to bounce around as I pleased. I did call my mom to tell her I'd gone to detox, but she didn't care. She was going to protect the kids at all costs and wanted concrete evidence that something had changed.

It was nearing Christmas time, and I was just empty inside. Everybody I was around each day was just living their lives, in a substance-induced coma, and didn't seem to mind that their lives had turned out this way. All I would talk about was getting back to my kids, and how God had a plan and was going to save me. Everybody was tired of hearing about my heartache and either I was going to join them in their misery, or I was going to shut up about any dreams and goals I had.

During these months, after appealing my unemployment case, I was granted unemployment for the ice cream parlor firing me without proof of intoxication. This money served me well and I was able to pay my way through the couch surfing I was doing. The week before Christmas, I bought my daughter a birthstone ring and, for the boys, hand-held music players. But I knew, deep within my soul, that if I was unable to see my kids on Christmas day, I would probably end up in some sort of real trouble. I called detox again. Surprisingly, they had a bed available two days before Christmas.

I left the gifts with my friend and told my daughter to pick them up. I can't remember how or who took me to get the Librium prior to this detox visit, but back to the pick-up point I went. It was James who was driving the detox van and I couldn't have been happier. I was drunk, really drunk. I jumped in the van and was relieved again to be anywhere but with myself.

This two-week stint was a breeze. I was familiar with the daily expectations and felt right at home. Christmas day, I was able to call the kids, but it was just the motions. I could hear the fear and the disappointment in their voices, and I could feel the coldness of my mother's tone.

This time, the staff insisted that I needed to go into residential treatment again. The program manager sat me down and explained to me that the best place for me would be the program I'd gone to after the intervention. I chuckled, "There is no way I'm going back to that place. Going back there would be like repeating kindergarten." What did they know? They had no clue what I'd lived through for the past couple of years. They thought they knew what was best for me, but their ego was obviously in the way of having my best interest at hand. I demanded to use the phone so I could get a ride out of there.

You guessed it. I called Charlie and gave him the address to come and get me. There was a strict protocol for families or friends not coming to the facility, but I didn't care. I was not going to go into treatment, and I didn't care who tried to stop me. James was off that day, so this was my chance to flee.

James had a way with words. He spoke life and love into everything and everyone he came in contact with. He always had things written down on index cards. During that stay at detox, he handed me an index card. It simply read, *2 Timothy 1:7 – For God has not given us a spirit of fear, but of love, power, and self-control.* I folded up this index card and kept it with me for the next eight months. I'd transfer it from pocket to pocket in whatever clothes I was wearing.

Charlie arrived to pick me up and I was determined not to drink. I had to try something else. Charlie had no problem adhering to my wishes and off to the dope man's house we went. It was New Year's Eve, and we were hanging out with the couple who lived up around the corner. They had deemed me the designated driver for the night as I wasn't drinking. I felt a smidge of progress. It was a facade.

Two days later I called the owner of the first sober living I had gone to after the intervention and asked if she had a room available. She was thrilled I was asking, and we sorted out the cost of rent and when I could move in. One of my friends who had been storing my stuff, gave me a ride to take my stuff and move in. This was a different room in the house than the first one I'd been in. This one had a bathroom attached to it.

I hauled my stuff into the room, introduced myself to my new roommate, and said goodbye to my friend. I used the restroom and when I walked out, there was my roommate, sitting on her bed, smoking meth out of a glass pipe. I gasped. I was floored. She looked at me like I was crazy and just kept smoking.

I started to put my stuff in the dresser and closet, and I felt like the world had just collapsed on my shoulders. I had come here for safety and retreat and now I was literally surrounded by madness. The next several weeks were some of the scariest times in my life.

It had now come to the point where the people I was around could feel the internal battle raging within me. It didn't matter what they thought of me. I wasn't going to settle for this life, and I certainly wasn't going to grow old, just accepting the bondage the substances and alcohol had trapped me in. I was not very pleasant to be around, but I was determined to find my way out.

Although I was drinking during these weeks, it was never the same. I had to make sure that I was safe at all costs. Each morning, I'd shower and head to the trolley, running for anywhere other than this fraud of a sober living. Within these few short weeks, I had managed to piss off everybody who had been so welcoming to me over the last year. My determination to find a better life was messing up their high, and they weren't going to stand for it. By mid-February, even the owner of the sober living told me I was breaking the rules for not being home when expected to be.

CHAPTER *16*

Another Desperate Attempt

I knew I had to make a big move and decided to go back to the treatment program I had vowed to never go back to—the short-term, women's residential program that I'd gone to after the intervention. I had asked a friend to drop me off there since there was such a wall between my family and me. The ride there was a complete blur as I was, as usual, heavily under the influence of alcohol. Upon arrival, although I did not want to be there, I gathered some cheer and presented myself to the intake staff as if I were home again. Staff that knew me from my 2007 stay said hello and then did a double take. They quickly identified the smell of alcohol on my breath and looked at each other to decide who would deliver the news to me that I was not going to be staying. I could tell by the look in their eyes that they really wanted to be able to help me, but there was no way they could risk "triggering" all the other residents in the program.

Once again, all hope was lost, at least for this solution. Stranded, with several bags of luggage, I called my dad. My hope was that he would take me home, I was just so tired. When my dad picked me up, even he was put off by my demeanor. As a father, and an alcoholic himself, couldn't he see how distraught this disease had me? And as a parent, wasn't he worried about the condition I was in?

Apparently not, because the next words out of his mouth were, "Where am I taking you?" As the car started rolling, the tears started flowing just as fast. I couldn't get the words out fast enough. "Dad, please take me home," I pleaded. Years of betrayal and abandonment came rushing back, and the thought of him leaving me, yet again, was almost too much to take. "I can't take you home, your stepmom wouldn't like that." Of course, I should've known it was always about my parents and their partners.

I continued to plead with him through the ten-minute car ride, and the more he said no, the more memories of his abandonment came flooding back. By the time we pulled up to my drinking buddy's house, I was so outraged, and he was so disappointed. I reached into the bed of his truck and flung my bags onto my friend's yard, screaming and cussing at him for never being there for me. It didn't matter, I was in this world of shit by myself, and it was only me that was going to be able to get me out of it.

CHAPTER 17

Hitting Every Wall

I mustered up some dignity and called detox, again. This time, although they had an opening, they told me that unless I planned on taking their suggestions and following through with treatment after detox, they weren't going to let me come back. I complied. It seemed that maybe they were right.

In thinking about going to detox three times within seven months, today I can define exactly why each took place. The first stint in August was out of desperation to live, the second stint was to be anywhere safe since I couldn't see my children for Christmas, and this third stint was out of complete determination to get on the right path.

When I arrived at detox, James greeted me so lovingly again. He greeted every client this way. He asked if I was ready to do things differently and assured me that doing things differently and taking suggestions would be the only way to maintain sobriety.

I went through the motions and was again a compliant client. As I neared the end of the fourteen days, we started to come up with a plan for residential treatment. They told me about this place out in the middle of the desert that was faith-based. They told me that at this place, you didn't pay rent or program fees for the time you were there. I would be able to save money and work on my relationship with God. Given the other options, I thought, how bad can it be? My plan was to save two months of the unemployment I had coming in and this could provide for a deposit for a little apartment or something.

The day had arrived to leave detox and there was a lady— a minister of some sort, who was scheduled to take me out to the desert. The detox van drove me up to North County and this lady and her husband picked me up. It was this couple who would drive me and another guy, who was going to the men's house, out to the desert.

The three-hour ride seemed long as we drove through unfamiliar roads. I felt like Hansel, mentally marking key roads and stores so I'd know my way back in case I needed it. We arrived at this row of manufactured homes out in the middle of nowhere around five p.m. The lady who came out to greet us was obviously familiar with the couple and they exchanged pleasantries. The couple and the dude with us drove off and there I was. Alone, in the middle of the desert.

They sifted through every piece of luggage I had, including each pocket of clothing. I didn't care, there was nothing there to find. Plus, I was on the road to better my life. When I went inside there were maybe ten ladies inside, and a few who were staff. It was wall-to-wall furniture with bunkbeds in each room. I put my stuff in the room assigned and requested the top bunk again.

The girls were making tacos and I offered to help. Stone-faced, the girl cooking told me I had to be there a few weeks before I could help prepare food. Odd, to say the least, but I remember saying, "I have to be here a few weeks before I can grate cheese?" Whatever, I didn't care. Two months would be no big deal. The tension in the room was thick. I tried to sit and talk with one or two girls, but they would not engage. I just assumed this was the norm for having new people enter their turf.

The vibe there was so off-putting that I told myself to go to sleep as soon as possible and that tomorrow would be better. Maybe they'd had a long day. I went to use the restroom and there was no toilet paper. I came out and informed them that the bathroom needed a roll of toilet paper. They all looked at me like I was requesting a bubble bath. The staff handed me four squares and told me I'd have to ask for toilet paper each time I needed it. Now this was starting to just get weird. But, again, what's two months?

I put on some sleeping clothes, crawled up in the top bunk, and opened my bible to the first page of Genesis. I'd start from the beginning as this was my new beginning. I fell asleep soon thereafter and was looking forward to being done with this day.

In the morning, I grabbed a cup of coffee and went outside on the patio. There were a few girls out there reading their bibles. I said good morning and was startled at the response I got. They looked up at me, but I couldn't see them. Their eyes were glossed over, and it was as if their souls were stuck elsewhere. Unless you've ever experienced someone's eyes being glossed over when they're talking to you, it is hard to describe.

I inquired about taking a shower and they went on and on about how this would be allowed in a certain order, basically after the day's work. I was totally freaked out by what I was surrounded by. I could handle being out in the middle of nowhere, I could roll with any program rules, but these people were in a trance of some sort. It was just weird and freaky.

I requested a supply of toilet paper, grabbed an outfit, and went into the bathroom to get dressed. I put my bible and sleeping clothes back in one of my suitcases and went into the main room. I politely asked if I could use their phone to call someone to come get me. Again, they looked at me like I was crazy. I can't remember why my cell phone wasn't working, it should have been, even though they had taken it from me upon arrival.

They informed me that I wasn't allowed to use the phone for any reason. I chuckled at them and said, "I'm not staying, I need to find a ride out of here." They went on to say that the nearest phone was at the store and pointed to the way I'd head. It would be about a half-hour walk, in the middle of the desert, but there was a pay phone there.

Fine by me. Even though I'd been on a very dark path for many years, one thing I knew was the Light of the Lord, and this was not it. I asked if I could leave my suitcases there until my ride came and they allowed this. I threw on my jacket, grabbed my purse, and off I went to walk to this pay phone. As I walked down this eerie street, I was so angry. I said, "Lord, I know you have a plan for me, and I know I've been dodging Your guidance, but I need for You to help me." I had walked maybe fifteen minutes when this old man pulled up to me. There was no traffic, we were out in the middle of nowhere.

I gauged his presence, and he asked if I needed a ride somewhere. I figured I wasn't the first girl he'd seen taking this walk down this road, but he seemed harmless enough. I asked him to drive me to the store so I could use the phone. We pulled up to the store and I scrambled for some change in my purse. I called my friend Ron who I'd just met a few weeks earlier. Ron had met me at the very worst of my existence and was always so kind to me. He didn't use drugs and only had a drink with me every now and then. I asked him if he'd come get me. He said, "You know it'll take me at least three hours to get there." This was fine and I was thrilled. Due to my Hansel instincts the day before, I was able to explain to him where I was. Ron would be on his way, and I'd figure out the rest later. The old man who had given me a ride assured me that I could wait for my ride at his house. He lived only a couple of houses down from the program. Again, I'm sure this wasn't his first rodeo with a wayward client.

I went into the store for a snack, and I couldn't believe it. The store was very big for being in the middle of the desert. The shelves were basically empty except for a few boxes of cereal and a few other items. But lo and behold, they had my kind of vodka and the mini bottles of 99 Bananas. It's another hard liquor that went down like candy. I bought a couple of each and got back in the car.

This would get me through the anxiety of waiting for Ron. When we got to the man's house, he explained that he lived there with his son. Gauging my safety, I knew I'd be fine while I waited. His son woke up and I offered to make them breakfast. It felt great to be around caring people. At least I could see their soul and knew that I wasn't in danger. After making breakfast and doing the dishes, I asked if he minded if I took a shower. He was fine with this.

Now, I'd been sipping on this vodka from the moment I bought it. I was terrified and sad that I'd agreed to this whole desert treatment stint. Either way, I was determined to find my way out of this cold, dark season in my life.

After the shower, we watched a little TV and I'd go outside to smoke. Hour two had passed and I was becoming more at ease knowing that Ron would be there soon. The old man and I talked about many things, and he was very kind and genuine. He had a car in the driveway that had a cover on it. I asked about it and he lit up. This was his pride and joy. He proceeded to remove the cover and tell me about all the work he'd done to fix it up. I can't remember what kind of older model car it was, but it looked fun and cool. He asked me if I wanted to drive it. Of course, I did. Anything to pass the time.

We drove this little race car up and down the street and had a great time. By this time, he had joined me in drinking. He had some beers in the fridge and was enjoying my company. I was checking the time quite often and although this man was so nice to me, I couldn't wait to get out of the desert.

Like a knight in shining armor, Ron pulled up. I said goodbye to this man and thanked him, whole-heartedly, for his kindness and hospitality. I got in on the driver's side and proceeded to go pick up my belongings a few doors down. My suitcases were sitting in the front. I threw them in the car and waved goodbye to whoever it was that was acknowledging my belongings pick up.

I drove down that same road I had walked hours earlier and found my way to the freeway. Within a few short minutes, Ron demanded that I pull over. I was drunk and he said he would do the driving. Probably better, I was exhausted and overwhelmed by this unforeseen path I had taken.

For the next few days, I would bounce around from friend to friend, just trying to pass the days. I knew something drastic had to happen and that I needed to be cautious with each step I took. Ron was always so good to me. He had offered for me to stay with him, and I did some nights. Other days I'd hang out with my drinking buddies and just ponder what my next move would be.

92

CHAPTER *18*

The Night in the Park

Mid-February 2010. This particular night, I just couldn't bring myself to go to any of my friend's homes. I walked around for a while, sat near the elementary school my children went to when we'd lived together, and then headed to the park attached to the baseball field the kids played at, across from one of our old houses. There wasn't much on that playground, but there was a kiddie climb that had an area to sit about five feet up. I climbed up into the playground equipment and sat. I was so broken and full of heartache. It must've been one a.m. by this time, and it was cold. I sat in the quiet of the night just empty inside, completely overwhelmed that it had all come to this. I remember, as if it were yesterday, the internal conversation I had with my Creator. "Lord, whatever You're going to do with me, just do it. I'm done. I don't want to do this anymore and I'd rather be alone than with anybody that'll have me." It was that night that the chains were broken. Although I would drink for the next several days, I never again got drunk or felt the same when I used any substances.

It was now March 13, 2010. I had stayed the night with my drinking buddy and slept on his couch covered in plastic. He, of course, still lived with his elderly father and they had furniture that had been covered for years in plastic. In the morning, as my normal routine I showered, dipped, and sat. It was a Saturday and I decided to call my sister. I was done and was going to step out of this life if it was the last thing I did. She was out delivering cookies for her church when I called, so I continued on with my morning. The fireman who used to live up the block from me had called, and off I went. Returning to my drinking buddy's house with a full bottle, I suggested we walk to get a sandwich. As we stepped out the door to go eat, my sister returned my call. She said, "No, you're not going anywhere, I'm coming to get you." It was a crisp Saturday afternoon. My sister showed up, with a friend of both of ours with her. I guess she needed some backup "just in case." I handed my friend my bottle and my weed pipe and left him a few dollars. It was always one of my worst habits, giving to others and leaving myself very little. That afternoon was the last time I would be in that old lifestyle.

In the blink of an eye, with one step in the right direction, my whole life changed. I had no plan or idea what was to come, but I took a leap of faith. I spent the night with my sister and my nephew. The next day, my sister insisted I go to church with her. After church, I wanted to nap, and I had a few Librium left from past detox stays. It scared my sister when I reached for one, but I assured her that it was only to take the edge off of detoxing. We made it through a second night.

The next morning my sister and nephew left for work. I was to be monitored by the same friend she'd brought with her to pick me up. Oh, the things that went through my head. I had left myself only five dollars. This would mean either getting on a bus to go back to the toxic environments I was familiar with or getting another drink. But not both. I called the faith-based women's home in North County that I'd heard about years earlier and the manager told me, "Be here by five p.m., we have a bed open." It was yet another miracle. My daughter and sister drove me up to the home that afternoon. We pulled into the driveway of a beautiful home up in the local mountains. This would be the start of a new life that I had only dreamt about. It was here, in this home, that God would heal me, from the inside out.

CHAPTER *19*

The Start of a New Beginning

About three months into the residential treatment right after the intervention, this girl had come into treatment. She said she had just come from an awful place. "They made us read the Bible all day and wouldn't let us talk to any men." I thought to myself, *That would be perfect for me.* But, of course, my pride didn't let me reach out those many years ago.

It was now March 15, 2010, and here we were, pulling up to this beautiful home in the mountains. We had stopped at the store for cigarettes on the way up and I'd grabbed a pack of toilet paper. I would bring my own just in case I had to ask for it again.

The house mother came out to meet us. As I pulled my stuff from the trunk, I grabbed the toilet paper. I'll never forget one of our first exchanges. "Do I need to bring my own toilet paper?" She looked at me with a puzzled look and said, "No, we have toilet paper." For many years we would laugh about this.

The Presence of the Lord was there. There's no other way to explain it but I could feel Him. I took a deep breath and knew, with every fiber of my being, that I was safe. I hugged and kissed my daughter and my sister goodbye. The house manager gave them the phone number of the house and told them I'd be able to call each day.

When I went inside, the women in the house greeted me and helped me get my belongings to my room. There would be a bible study at seven p.m., and I was okay with that. Dinner would be at five p.m., so I put some of my stuff away and joined the other residents in the dining room.

I had been through hell and had enough experience with other programs to know that this wasn't your average program. The place was clean, immaculate, and peaceful. At dinner time, we all gathered around the marble island in the kitchen, held hands, and prayed. There was nothing weird or freaky about these women or the activities we were doing.

We ate and chatted like normal people. They all were broken too. They were at a place in their lives where substance abuse had taken them to places that they'd never dreamed of, either. I felt welcomed and was thrilled to be there.

Each room had sets of bunk beds and again, I was comfortable to have a top bunk. They giggled at me and said they'd never known anyone to be so happy about a top bunk. They informed me that my bunkmate was at work and that she'd be home by eight or so.

After dinner, we all pitched in and did the dishes together. It was awesome. At Bible study that night, I watched the other women as they took their place in this cozy family room and soaked in the Lord's Presence.

I was home. It wasn't with my children, but at no time did I feel the urge to flee or run. When my bunkmate returned home from work, I introduced myself to her and asked questions like: What time are we allowed to wake up; what time are we allowed to shower; when do they give me a chore; etc. She looked at me puzzled and laughed, "You can wake up whenever you want as long as you're quiet, you can shower as early as you want and don't worry—in a couple of days, you'll get a chore." She reassured me that the main goal of this program was to strengthen my relationship with the Lord.

I couldn't believe it. That's it? All that was being asked of me was to settle in, gather my senses, and build my relationship with the Lord and my loved ones? Wow. Just—wow! This had been everything I had been striving for over the years. I had been dodging God's guidance for years, sometimes consciously, sometimes subconsciously. I didn't have any desire to go back to that old lifestyle or even see any of those old friends again. I prayed for them and thanked God for them. After all, they had been there for me when even my family hadn't been.

I called my mom the next day and she let me talk to the kids. I assured them that one way or another, I was going to make it back to them. Three days into being there, the house mother gave me my chore. My chore was to empty the dishwasher each morning. "The dishwasher and what else?" She laughed, "Just the dishwasher, the other girls do things, too."

I quickly settled into the rhythm of the requirements asked of us and was enjoying every minute of being here. It took me about a week to feel confident enough that I could get up and make my own routine.

Each morning, my bunkmate and I would sit at the kitchen table, one on each end, and read our books, Bible, journal and whatever else we were being led to do. There was such a Peace in this home, and I was soaking it all in.

I talked to the kids each day and although they were apprehensive, they would open up a bit more each day. It was enough for me just to hear their voices. This home had so many miracles happening each day and I knew my time had come.

Easter was a few weeks away on April 4, 2010. Some of the girls were going out to be with their families and some of us were staying in. This home provided everything from toilet paper to really good food.

We were encouraged to invite our families for an Easter meal if we wanted. I asked my mom if they'd be willing to drive up and eat with us. My mom and I were still walking on eggshells with our relationship, but the love was there. And that was all we needed.

I was so nervous and excited to see my children. Here came those handsome young men and I grabbed them and hugged them. They were just going through the motions. For many months to come, they would be apprehensive, hopeful I'd get it together but guarded in case I didn't.

My family was there for maybe three hours that day. During the meal, there was a significant earthquake in Southern California. We all gasped at how prevalent it was. But, one thing that didn't go unnoticed, was that we were all so thankful to be together.

Over the next several weeks, there were many other blessings that came with being in this home. This home had a child's room, and the residents could take turns using the room for the weekend and have their children come and stay. Since my boys were over eleven years old, the house mother thought it best if we didn't have young men in a house full of women.

Within the first six weeks of being there, I had earned enough trust from the staff that the house mother allowed me to go to my mom's house for the weekend. Every other weekend, my daughter would drive up to get me and take me to my mom's house to spend the weekend with the boys. She was now living with my mom too and going to school.

Things were so different. The chains had been broken and each moment spent with the kids was rebuilding years of dysfunction. The unemployment benefits that had been granted to me in November of the previous year were tailored, unbeknownst to them, perfectly for the current living situation I was in. I had just enough to pay my rent at the home, pay my cell phone bill, and a bit extra to spend on the kids when I'd go home for the weekend.

For the first several months I stopped carrying a purse. I had no need for one. I wasn't carrying a bottle around anymore. One day, my bunkmate took me to cash my check, and I pulled my driver's license out of my back pocket wrapped in a zip-lock bag. She laughed at me and said, "I'm going to buy you a wallet. It'll be a good start."

I took nothing for granted. Each day was like a new beginning, and I was getting comfortable with my newfound life. I could breathe, I was safe, my family was safe, and I was full of hope.

When first arriving at this home, along with my belongings, I also had that very large sack of baggage I'd been dragging around for far too many years. Little by little, the Lord would reveal to me another issue that was anchoring me to my old life. It was natural for me to take what I was being taught about Jesus healing all things and apply it to myself as He revealed these issues.

This was also a working program, meaning after your first thirty days, you could go out and find a job to cover your program costs and obtain self-sufficiency. I didn't need to do this. Again, the unemployment that I'd been granted from a previous relapse was covering any need I had. This gave me eight months to relish in the Peace and Presence of the Lord. This, along with seeing my children every other weekend, was just what my ravaged soul needed.

Soon after coming into the home, the house mother had stated that they needed a driver to take the girls to work, and drive to church both Wednesday night and Sunday morning. She asked me if I had a valid driver's license. I too, was surprised I still did, with all the years of drinking and driving I'd done. So, I soon became one of the drivers. It felt great to be a part of a community of women who were trying to rebuild their lives.

Another miracle was taking place as the weeks rolled on. The relationship between my mother and me was being rebuilt. We both knew there were years of hurt and shame that we'd both contributed to. We'd talk about things, sometimes fun and sometimes painful, like two grown women, and we'd move past them. We'd come to a point where we could talk openly, acknowledge each other's pain, and move on, not just bury the feelings of hurt and resentment. I had journaled for months about this. I knew, in my heart, that all those years my mother had stuck her nose in my business came from a place of true fear and protection of the kids. She had grown up with alcoholic parents and married a functional one with my dad.

Those actions of hers were to protect my children at all costs from dealing with an alcoholic. None of that mattered anymore. What mattered was that I was building a solid foundation that was only growing stronger as the days went by.

There came a time maybe eight months in, when my mom and stepdad were going to rent a different house a few blocks away from where they lived. Everything I owned, that wasn't with me at the home, had been put in a shed in my mother's backyard. She had gently approached me and asked if I'd be willing to go through the stuff, so they wouldn't have to take unwanted stuff to the next house.

The house mother had given me permission to go down two weekends in a row and I knew this sorting of my things would be painful. I would see things that at one time mattered to me and things I hadn't seen since the intervention took place. I prayed and prepared myself for the emotions that might accompany this clearing of things.

It was a lot of work. A lot of junk that could be thrown away. I had my dresser in that shed and a rat or two had made a home in the drawers. I hadn't worn those clothes for years, so it didn't really matter. There were the top drawers where I was able to salvage a few precious items like things the kids had made me, etc. Just recently, my mother showed me a letter I had sent her the week before this purge, stating my awareness of how much work it would be, and a hope for healing through the process.

Each issue or piece of "baggage" that the Lord would reveal to me, was dealt with. I was now sober enough to take responsibility for my part in them. I was now safe enough to let myself feel these emotions and work through them. I was now hopeful enough that working through these emotions that I'd stuffed for so many years was going to help me grow, spiritually, emotionally, and mentally.

It was everything I had prayed for. All those years of sitting alone in my room, drinking, racking my brain on how I could "fix" things, this was always my biggest goal. To be mature enough to take responsibility for myself and the amazing children I'd brought into this world.

I'm not trying to make this sound like it was all unicorns and rainbows; there were many tears that came with this process. Years and years of baggage being dealt with and many memories of how many times I had put myself, and the children I loved more than life itself, in very dangerous situations.

Eight months into the home, my unemployment benefits were coming to an end. I got a job at a local supermarket and was working as a courtesy clerk. This meant bagging groceries and retrieving shopping carts. Although there was some embarrassment that came with this, I was full of hope and happily walked through the next couple of months.

CHAPTER 20

A Tide Was Turning

During this time in the home, my stepdad had a stroke.

He'd had other serious health issues in the years prior, but this would be a drastic event that we hadn't planned for. He made it through that first one with minor effect, but then he had a second one. The second stroke left him more debilitated than the first. My mom was now dealing with raising two grandsons and helping a husband who needed constant care.

It was never my plan to move back home with my mother, but here we were with these unexpected circumstances. I remember one weekend while visiting the kids, we sat and had coffee and my mother was very nervous. She took a deep breath and started with, "I really need to take care of Alex, and if you would, could you move home with us? You can take care of the boys and I'll take care of Alex." This was so foreign to both of us. This was terrifying. All those emotions of hurt and betrayal came rushing back, for both of us, but this time, things were different.

Those chains had been broken and they had no power over us anymore. I went back to the home, spoke to my mentors about it, prayed about it, and it just seemed like the next step. It was all part of His plan. By this time, my daughter had moved out of my mom's house and was living on her own. There was an empty extra bedroom. As scary and unfamiliar as this move would be, I felt that it was indeed, the right thing to do.

There are a few things in this world that you can't stop; a dog that needs to pee, the Cartels, and God's plan for your life.

CHAPTER *21*

From the Ground Up

*M*oving back in with my family was scary and exciting all at the same time. I knew God was working and healing our relationships, but how would living together go over? Plus, there was the thought that maybe I was only staying sober due to being in a program. I was always a compliant client.

I made it home to them on February 13, 2011. It was the day before Valentine's Day, and I had bought a small present for each of my three kids. It was a Sunday afternoon when my daughter picked me up and drove me to my mom's house. I had nothing, no job, no car, no plan. But I had eleven months sober, and the chains had been broken.

We were all a bit anxious, but we settled in and had some dinner. The boys were very excited to have me home. They were still in the safety of their Gramma, and our relationship over the past eleven months was growing too. They were starting to learn to trust me more, but they didn't have to worry about being under my sole care, yet.

That first night was so special. The boys decided to pull out the air mattress and blow it up for me. They requested that I sleep in between their beds in their room. It was so touching. This went on for three nights and we'd giggle and talk about school, baseball, and anything they were involved in.

After the third night, I told them, "I think I need to start sleeping in my room now." Each morning I'd get them up, feed them breakfast, and take them to school in my mom's car. I'd then come back and help my mom clean and decide what we'd have for dinner. Things were going great.

A couple of weeks in, my mom and I had cleaned the whole house. She had mopped the kitchen floor and we were done. This floor had big, square tiles that were made of concrete or something to that effect. I came walking around the corner and slipped on the wet floor. My head hit the floor, hard, and there was a large cut on the back of my head. My mom was so nervous. We headed to the emergency room where they put a couple of staples in my scalp. She expressed to me that this was so scary for her. Her exact words were, "I didn't want you to start yelling at me or for this to make you relapse." By this time, we were able to express how we were feeling without all those years of trauma ruining everything.

I was not mad; I knew the floor had been mopped. I did not feel the urge to relapse, the chains and the desire to drink or use had been taken from me. That old me was truly disappearing as the days went on. I said, "I need a burrito," and we laughed. We had passed our first test of our new relationship and we were on a path of total and complete healing.

From here on out, being involved in the kid's day-to-day activities became natural. Going to their baseball games took on a whole new meaning. I was back, I was involved, and internally it showed. I didn't have that dread of having to leave them. I didn't have the shame of getting back on the bus, only to go back to a toxic environment. Things were changing, in every area of our lives, and I soaked it all in.

I was also very careful about my old behaviors. I continued to let the Lord weed those behaviors and baggage out of me. Things like being impatient, not being able to control what happens each day, the simple things that can overtake a person if you're not careful.

During the summer I had gotten a job cleaning out vacation rentals. These were gorgeous rentals on the oceanfront, and I'd make a couple of hundred dollars for a few hours of work. I started looking into going to school to be a drug and alcohol counselor. They offered these classes on Saturdays and there was a new class starting in August. I signed up, knowing I had enough experience in my personal life to last me a lifetime. Cleaning these vacation rentals was just enough to cover the cost of the school and I thought I'd give it a chance.

Each Saturday, I was in school from eight a.m. to four p.m. During the week I'd take the kids to school, come home and study, and clean a rental when a job came up. We, as a family unit, now had a schedule. My stepdad was getting better for a while, but then he had another stroke. My mom was free to focus on him and the whole family loved on each other day after day.

Two months into school, a job opening came up at the same detox that I'd been to so many times. I decided to apply and got the job. I couldn't believe it. Here I was, a year and a half later, with keys to this same building that had saved my life on numerous occasions. James had moved on to another position, but I was thrilled to be doing this work. The Lord had done so much for us. He had removed the obsession to use substances from me, He continued to heal the family dynamic and relationships that were so important to me, and now He was using me in the very places that were once a desperate refuge for me.

From here on out, God would open up the plan He had for me all along.

CHAPTER 22

The Chess Game of Life

I started working in Adult Detox one and a half years after being in that same detox. I had only been in school to be a certified drug and alcohol counselor for two months and it was great to be working and going to school on Saturday. My schedule was still wide open to tend to the boys, as I worked in the evenings. Day after day I would marvel at the fact that I now had keys to this building and was a sponge for everything I was learning.

Two months into this position, James contacted me and told me that there was a full-time opening at the teen center within the same company. He encouraged me to apply and informed me that he'd already told his boss what a great fit I'd be. I polished up my resume and sent it over to the manager of the program. Within a week I had an interview, and the position was mine.

My career was in fast-track mode and would continue to be for many years to come. Working with teens was a skill that took some time to learn. I had only been sober for twenty-one months at this time, but this didn't faze me at all. Although I didn't take a day for granted, I didn't feel the daily struggle of wanting to use, at all. The obsession had truly been removed.

I thought working with teens would help me with my parenting skills, too. It did, but not in the way I'd expected. Working with teens is tough. When it comes to addiction, at their age, they really haven't lost anything like children, jobs, homes, or relationships. They would get their phone taken away and maybe their video games, but the depth of addiction couldn't possibly be grasped by their young minds. I would always try to express to them that although they didn't think they had a problem, being in drug court at the age of fifteen was not a great thing.

I was very new to this field and to the counseling world. I would take what I'd learned each Saturday and apply it to my new position. My boss was amazing. He was a stickler for files and accuracy. He told me that your files represent you and if they are messy, so is your work. This was a perfect fit for me. I loved hard work, and I loved things in order. He and I worked very well together, and he'd give me tasks that I'd gladly take. There was some downtime in the first half of the day as the groups didn't start until the afternoon after the kids got out of school.

Early on my boss asked me if I knew what QAR was. Of course, the answer was no. He said, "You're going this month." So, four months into working in this field, off I went for a monthly Quality Assurance Review meeting. This is where a few different agencies bring their files and review each other's files for accuracy and compliance. I enjoyed every minute of it. I started to meet people from outside agencies, and I was fine-tuning my knowledge of what Drug Medi-Cal needed for compliance. All part of His plan.

At this time, we had an older man join our team and he was also a counselor. During the day, the three of us would get the work done and chat about life and many other things. This man had a uniqueness about him, and we became very close. He loved running the groups and I loved doing the paperwork, so it was a great balance. He'd giggle at me and tell me what a force of nature I was. This man became one of the dearest friends I've ever had in life. He too had been sober for many years and his wisdom and approach were remarkable to me. He was a no-nonsense type of guy and would tell it like it is.

In April of 2012, I had done my taxes and had enough money to buy a car. One of the baseball dads was going to the auctions and told me about the great deals they'd have each week. I gathered the money I had, and he took me to the auction. We walked around the lot; I spotted a car that was within my budget and in good condition and we waited for the auction to start. That afternoon I drove out of there with a car I had purchased myself. A car that would pass smog and that I had never drunk and driven in. I could feel the new habits I was involved in starting to bloom.

Now, as great as my career was going, my family life was going even better. My mom and stepdad were making strides and he was healing from his strokes. The boys were thriving in school and my daughter was pregnant with her first child. She had been seeing this man since mid-2010 and had brought him home to meet our family for Christmas, 2010. I'd still been in the treatment home at that time, but he was a gift from God. He was a good guy. Pleasant, smart, and kind, and he was wonderful to my daughter. He never saw me in my drinking days, and he was a great addition to our family.

In July 2012, my first granddaughter was born. Nothing prepares you for the emotions that come with having a grandchild. It was scary and exciting but by this time, I was able to walk through these emotions and be of sound mind. Blessings were flowing throughout all of our lives.

By December 2012, I won an award for Adolescent Outpatient Employee of the Year. It was a great honor, and I was delighted to have some stability building in my life. My family was truly starting to trust me, and the family dynamic was blooming in a manner that we'd never experienced before.

By mid-March 2013, I had expressed to the CEO of the company that my true skills were more administrative. I was getting a tad burned out with the teens and was fishing for what else was out there. She told me that there was an administrative position open at the Women and Children's Residential Program. I prayed about it, talked with my family about it, and I decided this would be a good change.

I ended up being the front desk receptionist at this residential program. Those eight months taught me so much and grounded me even deeper in my relationship with the Lord. The patience it took to deal with people all day long, at a very fast pace, was a skill I needed some practice with. Although each day was a test of my attitude and gratitude, I had a joy that was growing in me, and I took it all in stride.

I had been home for two years now and had established some really good boundaries and trust with my children. I knew it was time to start looking for our own place. The kids were hesitant and excited but knew that I was serious about taking the next step. Each week, I'd look at ads for places to rent and drive around the neighborhood I wanted to be in. It had to be somewhere near the school as the boys didn't drive yet. Up and down the blocks I'd drive just looking for rental signs. One day there was a 'For Rent' sign at this cute little complex a block from the beach. I called the number and they offered to show me the apartment. It was perfect. Two bedrooms, a window in the bathroom, a nice-sized living area and, you guessed it, upstairs so no one was over my head, just like a top bunk. One of the bedrooms had two separate closets and I thought it would be great for the boys. The realty company walked me through the application process, and I applied.

Within a few days, I got a call from the realtor that the apartment had been rented. It was a bummer, but I accepted it. I told God, "Okay, well now at least I know what I'm looking for." I continued to look but was not going to move to just any old place. Within a month, that same realty company called me and asked if I was still interested in the apartment. I guess the guy had been in the military and was getting transferred. I was ecstatic! I was learning that when the time is right, things fall into place. We moved into our own place in June 2013. It was the first place we could call our own since 2007!

Everything I had yearned for and had prayed for was happening. A job, my kids, my family, a place I could put my toothbrush, all of it. I took none of this for granted and was so very grateful. There were times, and still are, when I cry tears of joy as I'm scrubbing the bathtub. This may seem a bit extreme but when you've been where I've been, each piece of the puzzle is so very precious.

By this time, I was meeting people from all over the county. Other agencies came to see these clients in the residential program, and I'd chat and network with all who came through the front door. I was bored with my actual day-to-day responsibilities and would ask if there were any extra duties for me to do. One of the case managers from an outside agency was waiting for her client one day and told me about a position with her company. She said it was a dual role. It was part administrative and part alcohol and drug case management.

Once again, I sent off my resume and had an interview within a week. I can still remember being so nervous as I drove to the interview that day. I can also remember the song that was on the radio. Although I'd been sober now for over three years, I was still like an infant when it came to being an independent woman. I was full of hope and happiness and each step was exciting and new to me.

During this interview, I realized that this was going to be a really great job. The position was perfect for me. I could do the administrative work and go out to different locations within the county for case management. I'd be the floater case manager and would fill in when someone was on vacation, or the caseload was high.

This gave me access to many new avenues. This particular department served at six different county locations, and I would hop all around. It was fantastic. I was meeting people from all over the place and my responsibilities helped me grow and learn more about this field.

During the eight months that I worked at the residential program, I also started my weight loss journey. I had gone into the home at about twenty pounds overweight and had put on an additional forty pounds while in there. This was mostly due to now eating meals instead of just drinking vodka. I had made my mind up while working at the residential program that I had already put on my "recovery" weight, and they fed these women really well. I started with just salads and meat as a topper. I was also able to start walking as I was now home by five p.m. each day. At the teen center I wasn't getting home until 7:30 p.m. due to the classes being after school for the kids. Plus, I now lived a block from the beach so each day I'd come home, start dinner, and walk a couple of miles.

The pounds were coming off little by little. I found so much freedom in that short walk each day. I was shrinking on the outside and growing on the inside. Internally things were solidifying for me. I had built a sturdy foundation of people who would hold me accountable to my perspective on things.

Everything in life was new to me so it was like I was relearning how to be a woman, a mother, a daughter, a sister, and a friend.

In 2014, my oldest son graduated from high school. Both the boys were driving now, and my granddaughter was getting old enough to spend the night. I cherished every piece of my little world and was establishing clear boundaries for work and home life.

Many times, to this day, I can look back on all those years of sitting in my room, alone, crying and racking my brain over when this vicious cycle would end. I'd listen to music and just feel so empty and ashamed inside. I think about the people I surrounded myself with and my heart just hurts for them. As grateful as I am that they were willing to include me in their lives, it was all becoming so clear that God truly had other plans for me and my family.

This new job would be such a solid turn for us, both financially and spiritually. My integrity and hard work were starting to become how people knew me. My mom would always say that I was the most moral drunk she'd ever met. While working with the teens, they'd tell me stories about stealing bottles of liquor and how easy it was. Even in my darkest days, shaking so bad from withdrawal, it never dawned on me to go and steal a bottle. Either way, the things that mattered to me— love, family, honesty, and my most cherished value, sincerity— were surrounding my children and me, and we were growing into a family that had made it through the storm.

While working at this new job, I'd made friends with some of the people who shared the office building with us. There was a guy who worked in insurance in one suite and an attorney who worked in another suite. We'd take our breaks together and would laugh about life and business. This attorney had been sober for many years and in 2014 he told me about being on the Board of Directors for a men's residential program. He said it was nine men who were on the board, and that they could really use a woman's perspective. He asked if I'd be interested, and I thought, why not? I went with him to the monthly meeting one day after work and found myself to be moving to a different realm in life.

For the first few months, I felt like those nine men tolerated a woman being in their midst, but soon they started to value my opinion. We'd hold fundraisers every few months and I enjoyed being involved in such a great cause. Today, I'm Chairman of this same Board of Directors and have watched this program evolve and save lives over the years.

This was the year I also started working a second job. Many of my co-workers had second jobs. At first, the thought intimidated me. I thought, "Why am I working so much?" But in all reality, being in social service work is more about the passion for people than stacking money.

This second job was as a DUI Counselor. I would work two or three nights a week and the extra money was great. When I first started, the guy who was training me asked if I'd ever run a group before. Of course, I had. I'd run groups in detox, teen centers, and women's residential programs. After a week or two of training on the computer system, he told me I'd be running the group that Saturday. He assured me that he'd be in the room, but that he'd let me take the lead.

Running that first group, in a DUI program, I froze. I think I got five words out, "Hi, my name is CD Casa." All those memories of driving drunk with my kids in the car, driving them to school, driving around to the store, all of it, came rushing back to me and I couldn't believe here I was, teaching a group about safe driving.

But I was a natural. The thing I loved about these clients was that most of them were just normal people who'd had a drink and got behind the wheel. There were clients who were in the military, pre-school teachers, soccer moms, attorneys, and even famous MMA fighters. I could identify that small percentage of actual alcoholics and addicts in no time. I had picked up on the details of the computer program they used and could relate to these people so well. Most of them were so devastated that they were in any kind of trouble. I'd assure them that we all make mistakes and that sometimes things happen in our lives to fix underlying issues.

Every so often a piece of my story would come out but I never in my career highlighted the mess I'd crawled out of. I didn't have to. My job was to help them identify some areas of their lives that could use some tuning up and help them complete their program.

Of course, the extra money came in handy. By now, I was self-sufficient and would cherish being able to treat my kids to a family meal or buy my granddaughter a little treat I knew she'd love.

By now, I'd also started dating a bit, too. I'd meet men everywhere, as I was all over the county with my day job. My co-workers loved hearing my stories about my dating life. It was truly comical. I'd only been sober for four years at this point, but I knew what I would and wouldn't put up with. It was all practice. I'd go out to dinner with someone and say, "Thank you, I had a good time." Most of the guys that I'd date would take offense that I wasn't inviting them to my house or jumping at the chance to go to theirs.

It never crossed my mind. "Absolutely not! No, you can't come to my house. In fact, I hope you never find out where I live," was my thinking. I loved coming home to my peaceful little apartment. My children were safe and growing into young adults and we had built a safe haven. A new life, no alcohol, no substances, no yelling, no blackouts, no odd people coming over and hanging out. It was safe, it was secure, and I'd built it all with God's grace and my intentional decisions.

By 2015, things were just rolling along. I had gotten the hang of working two jobs and home life was fantastic. My third child would be graduating high school this year and he had plans to go to college in Northern California. Many new firsts were yet to come. I was also financially able to lease a new car by this time. My little brother, who had much experience with car sales, went with me to a few car lots and helped me pick one out. I saw two cars, exactly the same model, and for some reason looked in the window at the VIN number. One of them had my lucky numbers at the end and I said, "This is it." My little brother joked with the car salesman that I was a bit superstitious. It wasn't that at all. I just knew that this particular car was the one for me and that I'd be safe in it.

So many of my decisions at this point were made from my internal gauge of safety and soundness. It didn't matter to me what anyone thought. I knew that each decision needed to enhance my new life, or it didn't need to happen.

I drove this car off the lot with seven miles on it. As I followed my little brother back to my mom's house, I was very careful and scared. I'd never driven a new car. I was used to little beaters and this car felt so different.

This proved to be a great relief when the boys and I had to go for a weekend of preparation for my son's college. He had a test to take and a day of orientation. Although the school he'd be attending would be up in the Bay area, this orientation took place at their sister school in Los Angeles.

We'd planned for the weekend and off we went. I would still struggle with feelings of uncertainty regarding being able to handle these situations. But there's only one way to get good at unfamiliar things, and that's to walk through them. There were other parents, mostly couples, with their kids at this orientation. I was starting to get comfortable with just being me.

Next would come driving the nine hours to set him up in his dorm. My stepdad had a truck that he couldn't drive anymore due to it being a manual transmission. My son loved driving this truck so it would be this car that he'd take to college. The plan was to drive up, get him settled, and fly back with my other son.

I remember being so nervous about the whole thing. I was never good at long drives, and I certainly had no experience with college dorms. When we arrived at the college, my son found out where his room was, and we unloaded all of his belongings. I started to help him set up his things. His roommate came with his family –Mom, Dad, little brother, and sister, and they too were setting up their side of the room.

The feelings of inadequacy tried to creep in, but things were different now. These cookie-cutter families only appeared to be perfect on the outside and I knew that my years of darkness had built in me things money just can't buy. The kids always tease me about my behavior and sometimes, to this day, they'll roll their eyes and say, "You're so weird," but I was growing into the person I was destined to be, and it took a lot of concentration to walk through these new experiences. I'd been using substances since I was thirteen years old, and every new thing, through sober eyes, was terrifying and exciting, all at the same time.

Coming back home after getting him settled at college was new too. Just like when my daughter had moved in with her dad those many years ago, there was now an emptiness in the home. But, again, it was a different kind of emptiness. These were great strides my children were taking, and they were learning how to fly. I wasn't the scared little girl I'd been back then either, so we adjusted to life with a kid nine hours away. He was playing baseball in college too, and those feelings of not being at every baseball game tried to creep back in. By this time, I could identify situations that, back in the day, would make me drink. But the obsession had been removed and I was truly able to walk through these feelings and move on.

There were a couple of times that I'd fly up for the weekend and attend his baseball games. It was the same as when I'd take the bus from the sober living to his games. All the other parents knew each other and most of them were a two-parent family. I was different and I was okay with that. They had no clue what we'd been through, and they didn't need to know.

The relationship I was building with each of my three children was solidifying by the day. They were starting to see the results of hard work and determination and their respect for me as the leader of our family was starting to grow. I was sensitive to their opinions and their feelings. When things would come up, or they wanted to talk about things from the past, we were able to sit and calmly talk about it. My defenses and justification for my behavior had long been put to rest.

They now knew that the cycle had been broken, and they were free to grow into their true selves. They also knew it was safe to express how those years of my darkness had affected them.

The next couple of years were filled with excitement and stability. My son would fly home for spring break, summer, Thanksgiving, and Christmas. I would run around prepping to have him home like a mother about to give birth. I would stock up on his favorite food and drinks. And when he'd arrive, we'd love on him and enjoy our family time together.

In 2017, my daughter was pregnant again and we looked forward to welcoming another girl. Although the fear of your child giving birth doesn't get easier, my trust and confidence in God's great plan for our lives was much easier to accept.

Looking back over the years, I can see God's grace and how it saved us so many times. I was now seeing God's grace in my family and the strength that those dark times built in us. There's no easy formula to how we'd gone from there to here, but there are many things that I still do on a daily basis to continue the momentum.

CHAPTER 23

The Daily Grind

In 2015, the company I was working for in my full-time position was losing the contract to another agency. The new company interviewed all fifteen of us and hired six of us. This new company meant business with this contract and things were going to be different.

It's amazing how much you learn about a department when it's not being run correctly. Our old boss, although we always suspected he was under the influence, was nodding off at these big corporate meetings regarding closing the program. I didn't care. I was taking notes and unbeknownst to me, I would basically be handling the closing of the program.

All of this gave me great training for what was to come. We said our goodbyes and moved locations. This new company was very client-centered, which I loved. The majority of employees were women, which brought its own challenges. I did enjoy that the company ran its programs with integrity and honesty, so it was easy for me to settle into the new routine.

A little over a year later, the DUI company I was working for got a new contract to open up a co ed outpatient, smack dab in the middle of the hood. There was a great position open and since I was a tad bored with my current position, I decided to apply. The director was excited I was even considering changing companies and the plan was in place. In this position, I'd be the main point of contact for outside agencies and would be doing the Medi-Cal billing. It was perfect for me, and I was excited about the new adventure.

I'd need to switch DUI agencies to continue the second job, and this was pretty easy to do, too. The week before starting my new position, I decided to drive by the new office to see it for myself. This new office was exactly .8 miles from where my intervention had taken place ten years prior. I giggled to myself and was filled with gratitude.

This new position was a great learning experience for me. I learned so much about the ins and outs of setting up a new program and what it took to run one. For over a year we were growing as a program and a staff.

One day my new boss, who I really enjoyed working with, called me into his office to inform me that he was over it. He had put in his three-week notice and would be leaving the team. I was crushed. We had started this program together and we worked well as a team. Some things you just have no control over.

The new manager would be pulled from their DUI program. I knew this lady fairly well. We had done QAR together over the years and she was my supervisor at my night job. I also knew she was not someone I'd ever intended to work for on a full-time basis, but I sucked it up and continued to do my job.

In life, we have no control over how others behave. Some people continue to be shady and salty, and this lady was one of those people. She'd try to run the program with her fake smile and knew that we had to do what she said, whether it was working for the program or not.

I really did give it my best. Those few months gave me another chance to do some deep soul-searching and make sure what I was bringing to the table wasn't adding to the chaos. I could feel my spirit being tested on a daily basis.

My previous company had been asking me to come back to them. They had called and told me that my old position was open again and asked if I'd be interested. I thanked them but assured them that I was going to ride this one out.

By December 2018, I knew I was putting myself in a very tricky position. It didn't matter how much light and love I'd bring with me each day; the new manager was determined to snuff out any light and do things her way. I decided to go back to my old position.

The relief I felt when I gave my notice, although a bit sad that I wouldn't be able to watch this program grow, was just what the doctor had ordered. By now I had learned that home and work can quickly get out of balance if you don't first take care of yourself.

I was thrilled to go back to my old team. They were so welcoming, and I knew I'd made a great decision. Within a few short weeks, I was back to my happy self, and I continued to work both jobs. I'm not sure what the girl did who'd held my position for those two years, but everything was right where I had left it.

In no time, I had that department back on track and things were going great. By late 2019, our boss was moving and had put in her notice. We were sad to see her go, but happy for her and her family. By now, I'd gained great confidence in my abilities and was applying everything I'd learned over the years into my daily work.

I applied for the Program Manager position. Although the director said she knew I could do the job, there were some stipulations with needing a college degree. I was fine with that.

This would bring us to the great pandemic of 2020. In March 2020, we were all ordered to take our laptop computers and any supplies we needed and were informed that we'd be working from home. For those first few months, I'd work from my kitchen table.

My son had graduated from college in May 2019, and we were thrilled to have him home. He was now working on his master's degree at the age of twenty-two. This was my child who was brought into this world under such trying circumstances.

All three of my children, for having the parents they did, were shining in their young adulthood. The cycle had truly been broken. None of them have ever had any issues with addiction and they are kind, smart, and loving humans.

During the first few months of the pandemic, both boys were home with me. I'd make dinner and we'd enjoy meals together at the table. We made the best out of a really crazy time in life. The whole world was dealing with this pandemic and things were scary, to say the least.

In July of 2020, there was another Program Manager position open. I didn't think anything of it. That is, until the director emailed me and asked if I'd be applying for it. I quickly reached out to one of my many mentors and ran it past her. She said, "Yes, do it, they want you for this position." A bit scared, I humbly went ahead and applied.

I got this job and was just in awe of what the Lord had done for me over the years. Although many of my positions had set me up for running a program, it had never been official. I'd quickly learn what it meant to be a supervisor.

I'd use all the tools I'd learned over the years, and I knew that being a good supervisor meant much more than just the success of a program. To me, it meant dealing with people on a very humble level. I knew from all my prior supervisors, that boundaries and gentleness went a long way.

I was thriving in this position and had established a real groove in my home and work life. Within eight months, another position opened up. This would be running a women's outpatient treatment program. This position didn't interest me at all. I knew the hard work that came with this, and I was comfortable in my cozy little bubble. The director would talk to me about taking this position and I would try to avoid committing to it. This went on for weeks until she finally said, "I need you to move over to this other program; I need someone I can trust." Those were her exact words. Wow! All my years of making one good decision after another with integrity and truth had come to this.

The first week I realized that I had missed being on the front lines of helping people. A new excitement burst inside me, and I hit the ground running. These positions have given me great experience, and today I'm using my skills for productive, helpful work.

CHAPTER 24

The Nitty Gritty of it All

It may seem, to the average person, that all of this took place with very little effort. But, for those of us who have struggled with any kind of addiction, we know that there's a lot of hard work that comes along with changing your whole life.

I had avoided getting to know myself for forty years, and when God finally removed my obsession to escape reality, I knew that each step and each decision would be crucial to my healing. It wasn't just my healing that mattered, there were my children and my family that had been affected by darkness too.

From the second week in the home up in North County, I got up each morning, much earlier than others did, grabbed my books and my journal, and spent time with God. To this day, nothing happens in my world until I've spent that time with God. I don't miss a day. The very few times I have been out of town, I'd make copies of the pages for those days and take them with me.

I need guidance. Strong, secure, guidance. Although my family and my mentors are wonderful, I gain such strength from knowing that the Creator of the Universe talks directly to me.

I also journal daily. It's nothing fancy. I don't have those 5x7 journals with the fancy satin ribbon in them. I use the inexpensive, wire-bound notebooks from the superstores. I have quite the collection going. Each day I journal about things that are worrying me, new to me, things I hope for, and of course, my family's continued healing, happiness, and safety.

Today I know that God saved me to use me. This isn't something I'd set out to do on my own. All I wanted was to be a good woman, mother, and friend. But, over the years it's become quite obvious that the things I went through were meant to bring healing into all areas of my life and to help others find their way.

Then would come the part of taking responsibility for my actions. It's easy to hope that the freedom of sobriety would be felt by all involved, but that's just not the case. It was important to me to confess and apologize for things that may have hurt my loved ones. These things came at a much more rapid pace in the earlier years, but we've worked through them. I've found that the longer I continue to make good decisions, the less I have to go back and fix what I've messed up.

Today I can face myself and others. I've come to know that this thing we call life is a journey, not a destination. I allow myself to be led by the Peace I feel about a situation. I trust myself today and if it feels 'off,' I don't allow myself to engage in it. This includes people. It's another sad fact but sometimes we outgrow people. That doesn't mean we don't love these people, but we do need to be mindful about who we allow into our lives.

There are other things that I've done along the way to solidify my internal strength. The stuff I had in my mom's shed, the stuff that was so hard to go through, was one thing. I had moved all of my clothing to their new rental and there came a time when I needed to go through these too. This was early in my sobriety, but I decided to give away any and all clothing, including shoes, that I had ever drunk in. Basically, my whole wardrobe. Everything reminded me of a day, event, or person, and I just wanted to be done with it. It was very freeing and gave me a chance to enjoy each thing I wore.

Another huge factor I implemented very early on was that I absolutely wouldn't drink certain things. For example, I will not drink energy drinks, of any kind. There was a time when I'd mix my vodka with energy drinks in hopes that this would give me the balance I was looking for. Even the smell reminds me of the condition I was in. There are a few sodas that I won't go near because those would be my go-to for mixing drinks too. And we certainly can't forget any kind of cheap, fruity drinks.

Another thing I've learned along the way is the importance of self-care. Today I know my limits when it comes to exerting energy. I work hard, I love hard, and I also know when it's time to shut things down. Even when it feels like I should be doing something, I know when my body needs to rest. This doesn't have to be anything fancy either. Just a good meal and some basic television usually does wonders for the mind and soul.

I also exercise regularly. All those years of stunting my natural energy with alcohol were so unhealthy. You'd be amazed at what a good walk and sunshine can do for you! During the pandemic, most people were stuck in the house with nowhere to go. Today I'm aware of those things I need to do, both for my physical and mental well-being.

Most important is loving on my family. I would like to think that my children have reaped the rewards of my journey. Other members of my biological family haven't healed from their trauma. This doesn't give me the right to judge them, nor do I have any desire to do so. I pray for them, for us, and accept them for who they are.

I spend quality time with my children and my grandchildren. To some people, spending time with their family is natural, but for me, it takes intentional practice. For so many years, family gatherings were filled with resentment and chaos, so it took some time to unlearn old behaviors.

When it comes to work, although I love accomplishing tasks and being dependable, today I know that I don't need to impress others. The integrity and productivity I bring to the table show itself. I do love being a part of a great team, but I am mindful not to judge others who don't work the way I do.

I make a conscious decision to just let people be who they are. There are things that I can't control, nor do I have any business voicing my opinion over. If it's not affecting my little world, I can usually just let things be. This takes practice and patience.

Patience, oh that simple word that seems so easy. It's not. Today I've discovered parts of my personality that are just part of me. I know where my strengths and weaknesses are and I'm gentle enough with myself to allow myself to be human. This doesn't mean I excuse myself for acting like a jerk. I really try to approach things with a sound mind to avoid having to go back and apologize for mistakes.

There's still plenty of proof that I'm human. I do feel things, I do think things, and I definitely still say things. Not as much as I used to, so I am getting better.

Today I know that the seeds we sow, we reap. I have such a huge desire to believe the best about people, but I am also mindful not to be naïve. I was for many years. I'm sure many of those events over the years could have been avoided had I put all this into practice years ago. But we live and we learn. When we know better, we do better.

Life is in session and it's really all about our reaction to things. Sometimes we even get ourselves so worked up over a situation that never even happens. Our self-talk and our self-love are very important to our everyday life. They say that you can't love others until you love yourself and I find this to be true.

Boundaries and honesty are two things that I hold dear to me. I've found that people actually respond better when firm boundaries are in place. We can give of ourselves without losing ourselves.

These are just a few things that work for me. There is no magic formula. Unfortunately, what I've found both from my personal life and my professional life, is that addiction has to run its course. Just like the flu, it has to run its course. It doesn't matter what or who we lose, we have to come to the end of ourselves and just be done with it. This is a sad fact for those involved, but this is what I've found to be another truth.

My theory is that whatever brings you peace, tap into it. This could be anything from surfing, to yoga, to church, to Alcoholics Anonymous, or even knitting. There are so many things that bring us pleasure and peace in life but if we don't deal with the root of our issues and baggage, we'll continue to run from our true selves.

My hope in writing this book is that anybody dealing with any kind of hurt or pain, can open this book to any chapter and feel a glimmer of hope. If you still have breath, you still have a chance.

CHAPTER 25

From the Kid's Perspective

I have asked my children to write a couple of examples and memories of what it was like to grow up with a drunk mother. I asked them for the memory and to describe how it made them feel. I believe that this will be powerful in two ways. First, I want to be perfectly clear that things were not all rainbows and unicorns in our household. Most days were spent trying to ignore the elephant in the room. Secondly, I believe that writing these examples will be another piece to my children's healing. God has truly healed my family, but most things that people carry into their adulthood come from childhood trauma.

This is from my middle child, my first son, my rock of gentle and calm:

One day, after arriving home from school, my brother and I noticed that our mother had vomited in the narrow pathway between the couch and the wall. This wasn't the only pathway to the other side of the house, but it was that way or through the kitchen. Our room was on the left side of the house when entering the front door, and our mom's room and door to the backyard were on the right side of the house, so we frequently had to walk that way. I remember it took two full days before she cleaned the vomit up so in the meantime my brother and I would run and leap over the vomit pile so we could get into the backyard to play after getting home from school.

Physically, there were many times in my drinking career that my body was starting to shut down from the alcohol. There were times my eyes were bright yellow as if my liver wasn't processing things properly. I had discovered Milk Thistle by then and I would take this supplement hoping to "clear my system." There would be times when for several days, nothing would stay down except for a tad of Gatorade and the vodka. I threw up frequently. I was always trying to shake it off and tend to my state of being. I would also clean the house in hopes that the kids had a decent place to live.

As for this particular incident, I really don't know why I wouldn't have cleaned up vomit for two days. It's very possible that I was in a two-day blackout. This wasn't unusual. It's also very possible that I could have thought I'd cleaned it and done a very crappy job at doing so.

It's no surprise to me that the boys carried on with their daily lives during this event. They were such troopers. My older son was always his brother's protector and basically the most mature person in the home, even at that young age.

Before school one morning, I asked if I could have a friend over after school. We never had friends from school over, but I thought I'd ask. I was told it would be okay, so when I got out of school my brother, my friend from school, and I started walking to my house. When we got there, mom was asleep, which was normal. We went on to play video games or whatever, until she woke up and wandered into our room and promptly started yelling about friends not being allowed over. Even though I was sure she'd said it was fine that morning. I just assumed she forgot she'd given us the okay. It was a horrible feeling to watch him have to call his parents to come pick him up after he'd just experienced a total explosion that didn't really make any sense to any of us at the time. I'm not sure if I ever had a friend from school come over to my house after that day.

This doesn't surprise me at all. I was always parenting out of guilt, and I wanted to give the kids a life that other kids had. I had every intention of being a normal parent, every single morning. But that just wasn't the case, especially as the day rolled on. I'd be fine until about one p.m. and then I'd either need to sleep or I'd use some meth. Falling asleep in the middle of the day, and usually right before the kids were expected home, always made me feel terrible. I'd feel so bad that I'd failed again but there was no way to escape the slumber that was needed. If I had to guess, I'd say I was usually operating at a .20 blood alcohol level, way over the legal limit, and certainly soaked in an alcohol-induced state for a 5-foot-zero woman.

When I would wake up, I'd be very disoriented and ashamed that the kids had to come home to a sleeping mother, again. I can only imagine how horrified I was that there was another person in the home who had to witness what kind of a mother and home life my kids had. I had a secret I was trying to keep and having witnesses to my behavior was terrifying.

I'm sure that I acted like a complete maniac, and I can't imagine how embarrassing this was for my sons. As I mentioned in another portion of this book, people would leave their kids with me, but I know that these same people had lifestyles they were hiding too.

I have no doubt that my reaction to having a stranger in the house was full-blown panic. The thought of someone finding out what was really going on was too much to bear.

One weekend our mom asked us to bring her a peanut butter and jelly sandwich while she had been in bed all day. My brother and I went to make it but couldn't find the jelly, so we just smeared peanut butter on bread and took it to her. After a minute or so we heard her scream at us, "What, are you two trying to kill me?" because apparently it was too dry for her.

There were many days that I couldn't do anything but lay around. It wasn't really even about being in bed. Bed certainly wasn't comfortable for me, and I knew the stigma of "staying in bed" all day, was a very bad thing. But there were many times that I'd be so sick from the alcohol saturation that I couldn't get up and do anything. My heart was always broken knowing that I was a crappy mother and when I was sick, which was often, I was so worried about even making it through the next few days. I didn't intentionally rely on my children to take care of me, but when you have an alcoholic parent, that's what ends up happening. The way I talked to them when I was filled with worry is not excusable. I was fighting for my life, and they had no idea how bad it was. Although they had to deal with me, which must've been way worse than I could see, their presence was really the only thing that kept me hanging on, most days.

These next three examples come from my third child, my positive tox superbaby. All my children were saved by God's grace, much help from my mother, and the fact that the fight of my life built in them some really great coping skills.

You were drinking at the next-door neighbor's house, and my brother and I wanted to stop you. We jumped the fence and ran through the neighbor's house to stop you and then ran home. You came back walking up the driveway and could hardly walk. I thought we had no hope of getting the alcohol away from you.

There were always stipulations when I'd need to get my alcohol supply from outsiders. I always prided myself on the fact that I didn't do sexual favors to support my habits, but there was still a high price to pay anytime I needed someone to buy me a bottle. This was why I would try to make sure I never had to ask anybody for anything. My neighbor enjoyed hanging out with me and anytime he'd buy me a bottle, his thing was that I had to stay and have a couple of drinks with him. I didn't want to, but I needed the alcohol. I knew asking him for anything was going to be more of a hassle than it was worth, but there were times when I just didn't have my own funds. As we'd drink, I'd try to get through "the visit" quickly because I just wanted to be home with my kids. He knew I was trying to make the visit brief and I could see he would be offended by it. The other part was that people who didn't have children didn't understand why I wasn't harder on my kids. He'd say, "They're right next door, they'll be fine." I knew I didn't belong in his living room listening to loud music on any afternoon. I'm sure by the time I was 'allowed' to leave, I had consumed so much alcohol in a short period of time, that I was beyond intoxicated.

My neighbor didn't care what condition I was in. He didn't have anything to do but watch television and play with his dog. The guilt and shame and the amount of alcohol would always lay me flat out. Mentally, I knew I had 'parenting' to do, and I was failing miserably at this facade.

You had to work passing out flyers for Redbox or whatever and you were buzzed, I think. Your friend was babysitting, and you said there were drumsticks to be made for dinner. I was excited because of the drumsticks, and I said, "Oh yay, I can't wait." You took it as me being happy you wouldn't be home and started screaming at me. I just wanted the fried chicken without the side of screaming.

Oh, the years I was thinking I could reinsert myself back into the working world. This would've been back when Redbox was brand new, and nobody knew what this big electronic box of videos was. These machines were launched in the local grocery stores and the job was to stand in front of the machine and promote getting people to rent a video from the machine. Even though the gig was only once or twice a week and the shift was a four-hour window, I was in no condition to work, let alone drive there. I was very delusional in thinking I could "get out there and work."

I also knew that I didn't have adequate childcare. My friend, although he was trustworthy and loved my family, was hardly a responsible adult. I think he was around twenty-seven years old at the time and was still a child himself in so many ways. I hated leaving him in charge but again, I was trying to bring in some extra money.

Between knowing that I had no business getting in my car to go out in public and the fear of leaving the kids with my friend, I was a wreck. I would try to make sure they had everything they needed for a couple of hours in my absence. The fear, the guilt, and the uncertainty would cause me to lash out at anything that got in my path. My emotional intelligence was lacking, to say the least, and I had no idea that my outbursts would be affecting my children for years to come. There's no other way to explain these outbursts other than that I was just terrified with every aspect of my life. Spiritually I knew I should've just stayed home, but I kept trying to overcome the fear of getting back out in the world.

I think you called Q's mom a bad word. That ruined my friendship with Q. Q was my best friend at the time. I thought you were intentionally trying to make me miserable, and I started to just "wear" it.

Reading this doesn't surprise me either. I was never trying to make my children's lives worse. Having me as a mother was awful enough. But I also operated out of fear and guilt and was always hoping my kids knew how much I loved them. I'm sure Q and his family were nice people. My kids had a better gauge on people than I did for many years. I also had a secret to keep. The fact is, everybody knew, I could see it in their eyes. Again, my emotional intelligence was nil, and I would lash out to keep people away from finding out the truth of what was happening in our home.

While my kids saw me as this raging maniac who was keeping outsiders away, it had nothing to do with not wanting my kids to be happy. It had everything to do with trying to protect us. What a fraud! While my kids slept, I cried. I knew what I was offering for safety and stability was less than desirable, yet I would muster up some kind of courage to make it through each day. Maybe if I'd shown my kids how truly broken I was rather than trying to play it off like I had things under control, this wouldn't have affected them in the same way.

I know today that they can see that I'm a woman who speaks from the heart and is not afraid to confront my demons. I was this way back then too. However, my heart was broken, and my demons had total control of our world. Just like a marionette, every day was ruled by the bondage I was in, from the bottle.

These next examples come from my precious daughter, the one who witnessed more than any child should:

I was about four years old, and you and Charlie locked me in his bedroom and turned the music up too loud to hear me yelling to come out, so I think I eventually sobbed myself to sleep. How I felt: Worried, mad, and left alone.

Dating Charlie was a dangerous thing from day one. He was controlling and a narcissist. I never knew the extent of how much danger I was in, or the extent of the danger I was putting my daughter in until many years later when the kids weren't with me. Even in my darkest days and my drunkest stupors, I did everything in my power to protect my kids. This particular day, I had taken my daughter over to his house, which was the first mistake. I think this was in between us actually having a place to live so leaving wasn't much of an option unless I wanted to walk with her across town to a friend's house. I remember this day and his insisting that she mustn't see him using drugs. This part I agreed with, but I kept telling him that I'd sit with her while he did whatever he was going to do. His theory was that it was safest for her to be in his room, alone. As I did many times, I'd look for the next opportunity to get us out of there and somewhere safe. I do remember reaching out to Jack to come get us, but he was too busy with whatever chick he was entertaining at that time.

All of these stories from my children are so plain and clear to me today. Today, I would never accept this kind of treatment toward any of my family members. Today, all I can do is see the loving grace of God that covered us so many times.

I must've been about six years old. My brother was a young infant. You came home drunk and took a shower. When you got out, I was holding my brother because he was crying. Instead of comforting him, you were mad that he was crying, and you slapped his tiny leg. So then, of course, I was crying too. How I felt: Mad, helpless, and hopeless.

The only place I can think that I had gone, was to find Jack. I didn't really ever leave the house or leave my kids alone. But there were a few times that I'd hear the car Jack was driving nearby and venture out to see if I could track him down. That was always pointless, but I did do this a few times. I was always so busy trying to fight the feelings of anger and rage I felt towards Jack. As I'm sure I've mentioned in other parts of this book, I wanted the kids to know they were safe with me and that I was addressing these issues. I have no idea why I'd slap an infant's leg other than I was under the influence of substances and had zero control over my emotions. How terrifying for my children to have to live in that fear.

Around that same time, at about six years old, I remember waking up in the night and you had left my brother and me home alone. I had no idea where you were or when you might come back. I think I probably called Gramma. How I felt: Worried.

Again, I don't know where I would've gone in the middle of the night other than to think I could find Jack. At this time, I didn't have a car or friends so I wouldn't have just left the kids. I'm sure I was somewhere close but either way, how terrifying for my babies to have to wake up with no adult supervision. As I read these stories from my children, I'm overcome with gratitude that my children even still talk to me.

Several times I remember having to get in the car with you, way beyond the point of being safe to drive. The boys were with us too. One time you were yelling and screaming and swerving all over the freeway. How I felt: Nervous and scared.

In reading this sample from my daughter, it takes me way back to when she was an infant. She may not remember all of the terror we lived in, but I do. I was always trying to take us to a better place. Even before she was born, Jack and I would fight all the time. When she was very young and I moved out with her, I'd still try to go and see Jack and try to work things out. I'd always end up leaving in tears and swearing that we would never go back to him. As the years rolled on, especially once the alcohol had such a grip on me, I do remember the times I'd put them in the car and drive with them. For no other reason than probably being in a complete blackout, I'd suddenly feel the need to go "take care of something." What a nightmare for all those involved! I have no idea why or where we'd be going, but my thought was that I didn't want to leave them home alone.

When we lived in our first house out of the treatment program, you took us bright and early to the grocery store to buy a half gallon of vodka. We went home and I walked in while you were pouring almost a full cup for yourself. When I asked what the hell you were doing, you basically told me to mind my own business. How I felt: Disgusted and disappointed.

My sweet and smart daughter, and actually all of the kids, were always trying to keep tabs on the amount of alcohol I was drinking. Who could blame them? I was a mess. I would try every trick in the book—hiding the bottle in my room, in a drawer, on a random shelf, in the laundry room, anywhere other than the kitchen where they could find it. And, of course, when they'd catch me in the act, all my defenses went up. No alcoholic wants to be called out on their stuff. Again, my thought process at this time was nowhere near good child-rearing. My intentions were to be a good mother, but at this time in my drinking career, nothing was going to happen until I got that alcohol in my system.

While we were in that residential treatment program, we went to the zoo with some guy. I remember you having a drink with him there. I think I asked you about it and you tried to brush it off. All I could think about was all the trauma and crap we had already been through and there you were, doing that, at a place that was supposed to be fun for us kids. How I felt: Disgusted, disappointed, and now worried again that our life wasn't getting better.

Ah yes, the days of knowing that what I was doing was so wrong. The disease was calling me back over and over again. I can remember as clear as day trying to play it off like it was a normal thing to do. We were out for a weekend pass, I'm sure, and were going to spend the night at my mom's. This would've been the only reason I would be able to have a drink and still have twenty-four hours before we'd have to return to the treatment center. These red flags should've been a huge wake-up call for me, but unbeknownst to me, I would still be in bondage for another decade. How sad that my children had to experience this dismissive behavior from me.

CHAPTER 26

The Weeks Leading Up To My Breakthrough

Each year, as my sobriety date approaches, I go through this whole episode of where I've come from. It's a physical, mental, and emotional remembrance of those last, dark days. Physically, my body can feel that there was a bondage that held a grip on me, and it can remember just how weak and sick I was. In the last weeks of my old life, surprisingly I wasn't alcohol sick, but I had been many times during my drinking career and knew it was always lurking around the corner. Mentally, I can recall like it was yesterday, how sad and scared I was. All I ever thought about was my safety and that of my kids. I'd lie awake at night, tossing and turning, on whoever's couch I was sleeping on, formulating a plan to make things better. To break free from the ongoing nightmare. Emotionally, I can still remember those dark forces that were trying to persuade me that my life would never get better, that I'd never reside in a home again with my babies, and that all those hopes and dreams I once had, were way too far to be reached.

I used to have a little 5x7 daily planner that I carried with me in those last, dark months. It fit perfectly in my purse right next to my bottle, and I would jot down every little detail of my day. For example: *Went to so and so's house with eggs and chorizo hoping to make some food and have a good day. They started fighting an hour into being there, so I ate and left. Went to so and so's house and they were sleeping so I sat and watched television for a while. So and so called and picked me up and went and did my laundry.* Just complete and total nonsense. There was nothing productive happening with my days and I was running from each toxic situation only to find a minute of solace in another shady environment.

I'm not sure what happened to that planner. I may still have it in a storage bin, or I very well could've decided around my sixth year that I wanted to be rid of it. I do not need the book to remember the despair and desperate state of my life in those last days.

I'm writing this portion of my book on the eve of my sobriety date. Tomorrow it'll be eleven years since I have touched any substances or been in those toxic environments. By this time, in those last dark days, I'd been staying the night at either my drinking buddy's house or Ron's house. It was easier to hang with my drinking buddy, as he lived with his father who was a very old man. Plus, my drinking buddy would be too drunk by eleven a.m. to be concerned about my stress level. He and his father would do everything possible to make me comfortable, but there was no comfort to be had. His dad was always so nice to me. He was a lonely old man and was beyond frustrated with his grown son being a drunk in his home. When I would be there at his bedtime, he'd bring me out a pillow and blanket and say, "Now lock the door and get some good rest." It was very sweet.

The pillow and the blanket were always as thin as a bed sheet. Their furniture was still in the condition they had bought it in over forty years earlier and was covered in plastic. I guess back in the olden days, people would cover their furniture in plastic to preserve it. I'd already wiped down my targeted area of the sofa on numerous occasions and always slept in my clothes so "getting comfortable" externally, and internally, were just about on the same level—non-existent.

The night before I called my sister to come get me was one I'll never forget. It was March so it was cold outside. My body felt pasty and sticky from the alcohol saturation, but it was too cold to take off any layers of clothing. I slept in my jeans and always kept my hoodie on. The only comfort I could give myself was to pull the hood over the back of my head to try and relax into what I knew was a clean garment.

I took my shoes off and gently lay myself onto the plastic-covered couch. I propped the pillow against the armrest hoping to enhance the pillow. I pulled my hood over my head and positioned myself for rest. I didn't have enough alcohol on me to drink myself to sleep, so there I lay, sweating, heartbroken, worried, and determined to get out of this shithole I had dug myself into.

As the night rolled on, I may have dozed off for fifteen minutes here and there, but every time I moved, the plastic and despair would wake me right up. I could see my children's faces in my mind, and I could hear their precious voices and laughter and I would yearn so deeply to be with them.

I've always been an early riser and this night was no exception. I remember sitting up and looking out the front window. My deepest hope was, "Lord, please help me, please don't let this be the end."

By the time my drinking buddy woke up, I was showered and ready for anything other than sitting on that plastic couch. I had no idea that my breakthrough was happening that very day.

What I know today is that at my weakest moment, God had a plan. We should never try to guess what God's next move will be because we may totally be off the mark.

140

CHAPTER 27

A Few Stories The Kids May Not Remember

This had to be 1997, after I'd had my third child, those few months in between having a positive tox child and getting some help. Jack's brother would often come visit and would tell me all about his secret life. He would tell me about these explicit underground sex shows he would go to and the people he'd meet there. Knowing he was married, and being intricately woven into this family, I would listen and laugh as he explained that he did it all for the thrill. He would also tell me that I could make a lot of money being involved in this lifestyle. Of course, I knew I wasn't going to delve into that lifestyle, but I decided to go out with him one night just to get out of the house.

I believe my niece was babysitting that night, as she had a few times before. Since I never left the house except for groceries or to take my daughter to school, getting ready was foreign to me. He came to get me and off we went to a strip club. Back in those days, alcohol hadn't been a major factor, or at least I thought it wasn't.

We were at the strip club for an hour or two and drank and mingled with the girls who worked there. He kept telling me how much money was to be made in these jobs and seemed to be familiar with the staff. One of the girls kept asking me to go home with her but I laughed it off, knowing all I really wanted to do was go home.

I can't remember the drive home that night, but my maternal instincts must've been prevalent in my soul. He dropped me off, walked me upstairs, and asked if I'd be okay. I assured him I would and off he and my niece went.

It had to be three in the morning or so, and since I hadn't remembered the drive home, the whole thought process was blurry. I was in a blackout. I do remember running the bath water to give the kids a bath. My precious daughter was eight and my son was a year and a half old. I woke the kids up and gave them a bath in the middle of the night. I dressed them for bed and here's where the memory, although vague, comes back to haunt me often.

I guess I decided to take a bath too because the next thing I remember was my daughter telling me over and over, "Mom, wake up. You're falling asleep in the bathtub. Mom, you've got to get up." She was very persistent and I'm sure she was unaware of the severity of this ordeal. After several minutes of her persuading me to get out of the bathtub, I guess I must have, because I'm alive today.

I know, without a doubt, had she not been there, I would've drowned in the bathtub that night. These precious children of mine have saved my life on more than one occasion. Left to myself, I have no doubt that the intensity of my despair would've unintentionally gotten the best of me.

Another heartbreaking story is the time we came home to find Jack outside with some dude. This very well could have been that same four-month period between having my third child and getting help. The devil was trying to stop God's plan for us, and I should've been on guard. But I was lost in the hopelessness surrounding me.

I walked up with the kids and Jack was with some guy I'd never seen before. They were standing by this guy's car with the hood open, so I didn't think anything of it. Jack was very skilled at fixing cars and other things. Of course, that never covered anything in our lives that needed to be fixed, but that didn't mean he didn't help other people.

I took the kids upstairs and within a few minutes, Jack came inside with this guy. I had no clue what was going on. They made their way to the bedroom, and I was ordering pizza for the kids. I didn't question Jack's actions. By this time, any time he was home was enough for me to feel even a little bit safe.

The pizza arrived and I fed the kids. I cracked the bedroom door open to ask if they wanted some pizza. They both said yes, and I served them a plate and went back into the living room with the kids. All was well. Or at least I thought.

Maybe an hour later, they emerged from the bedroom and Jack informed me that he had to leave with this guy. I urged him to stay with us, but it was futile, as he never stayed with us.

When Jack returned days later, he scolded me for being so nice to that guy. He yelled at me, "That guy was holding me at gunpoint because I owed him money, and you were offering him pizza. The next time I'm having a conversation with somebody, mind your own business."

"Mind my own business? Oh, hell no. How about if you stop bringing all these dangerous people around us? Why don't you get a job?" That was all it took for him to build his case and leave again for several days.

I can't imagine all the dangerous situations we were put in without having any knowledge. The thought of what could've happened that day infuriated me and made my will to fight even stronger. Another example of the many times God's grace and mercy were covering my family without me even knowing it.

Another story that will always haunt me took place in the last house we lived in. This had to have been 2006 and it was just the boys and me by this time. The boys were into skateboarding and my son wanted new wheels for his skateboard. I was sitting at the kitchen table with the phone book in front of me, calling different places to find out who had these wheels. The boys were buzzing around me with energy and excitement about putting these new wheels on the board.

I was half-ass calling these places as I knew I didn't have the money for them. The first few places I called did not have the wheels, which was fine by me. Even if they had, we weren't going to get them that day. I didn't have the money and I was way too intoxicated to get in the car. I couldn't bring myself to tell the kids that this wasn't going to happen, and I played the part of searching for said wheels. I don't remember what my son said, but out of shame and guilt I pushed the phone book across the table, and it hit him in the chest. He was shocked and sad. They trotted off to their rooms, knowing that the wheels would come another time. I was crushed. I never hit my kids, not intentionally, but this memory of that heavy phone book, flinging across the table and connecting to his little torso, can still bring a tinge of sadness. I cried for hours thinking of what an awful mother I was. This was all building up to the insurmountable months that were headed our way.

CHAPTER 28

From There to Here

As I mentioned earlier, there is no magic formula to how I got from there to here. Today I can look back at the possible reasons for all of this madness and only identify what my truths are. I know today that what worked for me may not be the solution to everyone's problems. I also know that what works for me can be accelerated and fine-tuned to continue to be a pathway for healing.

Let's start with the alcoholism itself. I am not a doctor, but I believe it is genetic. It got passed down from my ancestors and those who came before me. There's another term for these genetic issues, called generational curses. Either way, it comes from the genes we were born with. I know, without a shadow of a doubt, that I come from generations of alcoholics, on both my mother's and my father's side of the family.

What they did with their alcoholism was played out in many ways, but I believe I broke the cycle. It's amazing to think that I had no idea this would be the case, but it surely is what has happened.

My children, although they have the genes, have lived and witnessed this inherited trait and have rock-solid information on how not to let these issues overtake their lives. I enjoy watching and knowing that my kids are able to have a beer—one beer—while watching a baseball game. Or having one beer after a long week of work. Somehow, through all this mess, they have turned out to be emotionally, mentally, and physically stable young adults.

Although I was aware of these generational genes, I wasn't emotionally or mentally stable enough to guard myself against the factors that contributed to my explosion of alcohol use.

Today I can look back on the early days of babysitting for a neighbor and raiding the liquor cabinet. Or the early years of dealing with Jack when my go-to would be to buy a six-pack of beer. Or the early rounds of treatment when I was sneaking a drink. And, of course, the early part of my drinking career when I was hiding bottles. All of these things should've been huge red flags, but again, I was destined to go through this to break the cycle for the next generation.

Moving on to the abandonment issues. These started at a very young age, for sure as early as ten years old when my parents got a divorce. The giant hole this left in me as a young girl was a trap waiting to be filled with something, anything, other than the pain I felt. I know my mom tried to make things good for us, and they were in many respects, but that pain of having the person who's supposed to be protecting you ripped from your life is something that every parent should address at the heart level. Many things, including therapy, would've been a good start to repairing that gaping hole in a little lost girl. I'm sure my sister and I would've shrugged it off as ridiculous, but who knows, it may have been a step to redirecting my path.

I'm a firm believer in everything happening for a reason so I wouldn't change any part of my story. If my madness saved my three children and the generations that follow from having to repeat the same mistakes, then let it be me, Lord!

Even things as simple as talking about the hurt that comes with divorce might have helped with these extreme feelings of abandonment. But I then chose a man who would do exactly the same thing, to the hundredth degree.

I was too young and engulfed in treading water throughout my life to have caught this myself. They divorced and we went on. Or so we thought. Had I been emotionally mature enough, I may have been able to ward off any type of circumstances that would come my way. But I wasn't and I fell into that trap head on.

Now for the bitterness. Oh, what a bitter child I was. This bitter child grew into a seemingly normal adult. Nothing could be farther from the truth. I was emotionally and mentally damaged. I dragged this gaping hole of hurt with me into adulthood and it only grew bigger as I allowed people and situations to affect me. I had no clue that the case I was building was only harming myself.

Today I don't allow any form of bitterness into my life. Oh, it tries to come at me, no doubt. But I'm aware of things that make me bitter, and I don't partake in letting them into my world.

Resentment – a noun defined as bitter indignation of having been treated unfairly. Life is unfair, most of us know this. But it takes years of undoing if it has wrapped its web around you. I was resentful of so many things. My dad, who was emotionally unavailable my whole life, my parents' divorce, and my mother, who started dating around in my teen years, and left me to care for my little brother quite often. My sister, who never protected me as her younger sister. Friends who cheated with my boyfriends in high school. Once Jack entered the scene I had a whole new list of things to be resentful about: him never having a steady job, him never being emotionally available to me, and then the kids, him out cheating with every chick who would accept his behavior.

Then came the resentment of having to raise the kids on my own. There has never been a day where I felt like I wished they weren't in my life. They made life better and they were my world, even though I was failing miserably at showing this.

Again, today, I don't allow myself to do things or let people do things to me, that might make me resent them. Somehow, over the years, I've built firm boundaries and I stick to them. That's not to say that I'm not flexible; I am. I just know my limits, give things my all, and also know when it's time to cut the cord on any given situation that is sucking the life out of me.

There are two other aspects of being an alcoholic that must be mentioned—shame and guilt. Shame is one of the most damaging characteristics in any person's life, yet for the alcoholic, it comes in excess with every sip taken. In the beginning cycle of any alcoholic's stint, the drinking feels like it's helping to cope with life. It feels like an elixir that is helping to settle the chaos within. It feels like something that can be controlled, and for the alcoholic, we really believe that, in the beginning. But there comes a time, and I truly believe no alcoholic can pinpoint this event, when the alcohol makes a shift.

It's an unspoken, invisible shift that happens within, and suddenly, the alcohol has all the control. Physically, the body starts needing it and mentally we accept it, wanting to believe wholeheartedly, that we are still the one in control.

It's a sham, and this is where the shame comes to stand and pound its chest, if you will. I can only speak for myself, but this shame of being so dependent on a liquid comes with many tentacles attached to it.

It's unbearable to think that something so obvious can have so much control over you and the feelings of worthlessness that come with it are too much to bear most days. There are the revolving thoughts that come along with this, that somehow, we can take back control. All the while, the intake of alcohol increases. For me, I would roll this around in my head, day after day, and night after night, that if I could just control how much I was drinking, things would get better.

There's the shame of hiding it, or at least attempting to, from everybody near and dear to us. If they truly knew how much I was drinking or how lost I was in this battle, there would be dire consequences. It all comes out in the wash eventually.

And the guilt. What a sad emotion to live under every day. I think the only thing I ever felt guilty about was being a shitty mom. But being a good mom was the only thing I wanted to be so this was the worst thing for me. I wanted so badly for my children to know how much I loved them, but all of my actions showed just the opposite. I felt so bad for the circumstances I had allowed to overtake our lives. I did a lot of my parenting out of guilt, and this was always a double-edged sword.

I knew that I had nothing to offer them and by the time I'd get it together mentally and decide I was going to change this, the alcohol had me in such bondage that nothing I did was long-standing.

Those were the feelings that I lived under for many years. It was a long, hard road, and sifting through all of these years of emotions once I was sober took some work. All the hard work has definitely been worth it. Today I can use all those years of turmoil in my everyday life. It makes facing any challenge that comes my way a pleasure to walk through.

There are two other emotions and firm beliefs that I lived under through all those years of darkness, and these were, and are, my hope and my faith.

Through all the years of living in extreme chaos, I always had a hope that things would work out, eventually. I had, and continue to have, a hope that is larger than life. I can remember people that I'd hang out with telling me to stop talking about being home with my children and stop talking about God. They'd assure me that I was living in a fantasy world and that I'd never make it home to my children. I'd brush it off because deep inside, I knew the day would come when I'd crawl out of this hell hole that I'd built for myself.

Even as a young child, I could feel a well of hope burning inside me. As terrified and traumatized as I was as a young girl, I knew that there was another side to life that I'd eventually make it to if I could just hold on.

In my years of early motherhood, shaking my head at the extreme set of circumstances I'd created for my children and me, there was always that hope that things would work themselves out. I'm so truly grateful that I was able to hang on. That I was able to see the good in life that I so desperately wanted. That I held on to this hope, this passion, this yearning for a better life.

And my faith. This too, I've had since as early as I can remember. Although we'd attend church on holidays when my parents were married, this isn't where my faith came from. And once my parents divorced, my mom would take us to church nearly each week, to instill in us a Higher Power that we could look to.

But that's not where my faith came from. Somehow, I've always had a deep connection to the Creator of the Universe. A connection as deep as the ocean and as high as the mountains. A connection so unique it used to scare me. I don't like labels, so I don't consider myself religious. But I can say, without any hesitation, that I have an intimate relationship with the Lord of my life.

Today I tap into this connection on a daily basis. I start my day with this connection, and I write myself notes to remind myself during the busyness of the day, that there is Something much larger than me in charge of this thing called life.

I don't expect or demand anyone to understand my faith. I don't need to explain myself or my beliefs to anyone. But it works for me. I find great comfort in knowing that there's an All-Knowing Power out there that I can turn to, at any given moment, and get guidance and clarity, for any situation life may throw at me.

CHAPTER 29

The Final Outpouring

Each morning, while reading through my devotionals and journaling, I get grounded in the Word of God, which is how I choose to start my days. For weeks, I'd been stuck on how I would finish this book, and second-guessing myself on what I'd already written.

One morning recently, one of my devotionals read that what is secretly in our hearts is expressed through our words, our facial expressions, and our attitude. It went on to say, "What would your song sound like today?"

Life is in session, and with all the stressors surrounding work, home, and this worldwide virus that had been going on for so long, driving to work that morning, I spoke, out loud, "What my song would sound like today."

The reason for writing this book was to extend hope and help to any others who may be struggling with things that are just binding to the soul.

It was there, in that moment, that I realized that this would be how I would wrap up this book.

My song would go something like this:

Lord, I thank You. Thank You, thank You, thank You. You are my God, and I am Your pretty princess. You alone Lord, have done all of this for me, for us. None of this could have been possible without Your protection and Your guidance.

I thank You Lord for the passion, perseverance, purity, and peace You've instilled in me to walk through this life. I thank You Lord, for your continued hedge of protection over me and my family.

Lord, I trust You and I believe that You will continue to cover and prosper my precious V.L., A.E., R.R., E.F., my MAG1 & MAG2. My mom and A., my dad and R., my sister, J., J. and R., L. & L., my little brother and L., A., W.

I would continue on with each extended family member, friends, co-workers, associates, clients, neighbors, and anyone I come in contact with.

I think this is the most spiritual side I've shown to those who are reading this book, but it needed to be done. My kids sometimes throw out the word "religious," but I don't consider myself religious.

I have no opinion on what your beliefs are or how any person should conduct themselves. I just know that for me, I have a deep, personal relationship with the Creator of the Universe.

My song would go on to claim all the promises God has for me and my family. I claim absolute healing, power, and restoration; I claim blessings overflowing in our lives.

I ask Him to use me, to help those I come in contact with to feel His Peace, through me. I know, without a shadow of a doubt, that nothing I face today could ever paralyze me the same way my days of darkness did.

For those who may be struggling, my suggestions are simple:

• The first question is always the most important. Do you want to be free? Do you really want help? So many times, people will ask me things about services available to get help, either for themselves, a family member, or a friend. My first question is always, "Do they want help?" Sometimes people like to stay stuck in their mess. Or the thought of working through the deep-rooted problems is so overwhelming that it's easier to stay stuck. But, if you truly want to get better, there are several ways to get there.

• Tap into what gives you peace! This could be yoga, church, surfing, knitting, self-help meetings, etc. Whatever it is, tap into it. Go after it. Get up and try it. If it doesn't work, try something else. Whatever you do, don't continue to sit and sulk in your mess. Start with a ten-minute walk. Do something to change your scenery and state of mind.

• Get help! There are so many resources today for those who are struggling. Free help is available, at your fingertips. But, you'll have to take that first step to getting there. What's the worst that can happen? If you find that you actually enjoyed sitting in the pit of mire, you can always go back. One thing about a messy, distraught lifestyle is that it's always there for the taking.

• Write down your feelings on a daily basis! When we write things down, pen to paper, we'll find that our behaviors have patterns. Our feelings have patterns. The way we react to situations and our responses, sometimes even to those we love the most, have patterns. Letting this stuff roll around, over and over, in your head and your heart, is maddening. Write it down. Don't be worried that someone is going to read it. If you fear someone may find out what you're really thinking, then maybe focus on your boundaries of getting these people to respect your privacy.

• Boundaries—set some! People respect boundaries. There are those who won't set boundaries and get more from us when we don't set any boundaries. Start with little things like saying no when you truly don't want to do something. Or not continuing a relationship that doesn't bring out the best in you. Boundaries should be set in all areas of life but start with the basics.

• Dream big! It's not too late to have those things you've always wanted. Even if you only get half of it, it's better than dreaming small and getting all of it. If you've always wanted your degree, pursue it; if you've loved someone for a long time but keep waiting for the right moment to tell them, do it now; if you're stuck in a job that drives you crazy, plot out a new plan. Life is too short to live it in misery.

- And finally, be gentle with yourself. We are a lot harder on ourselves than we are on the people around us. We put expectations on ourselves and our behavior and then beat ourselves up when we don't meet our own expectations. I've found that for most of us, as tough as we are, we are very sensitive people. Start small but be kind and gentle with yourself. Give yourself a break! It will end up having a trickle-down effect,; you'll then be able to approach the world around you in a kinder, gentler manner.

- Finally, be kind, keep the faith, and never give up!!

Thank you and I hope you enjoyed reading through my journey.

Sincerely,

CD Casa

About the Author

CD Casa is a fun and witty woman who was born and raised in Southern California. She has worked in the Behavioral Health Field for over twelve years, educated both in school and the school of hard knocks. She's learned, both personally and professionally, that most things have to run their course and that it's about the journey, not the destination.

Learn more at:

cdcasa.info

instagram.com/cdcasa2023